Portrait of the Artist
with a Young Dog

Stephen Claypll

slchap6283@gmail.com.

Portrait of the Artist with a Young Dog

Poetic Outbursts, Mainly About Puppies

Stephen Chappell

Portrait of the Artist with a Young Dog
Stephen Chappell

Designed, printed and bound by Aspect Design
89 Newtown Road, Malvern, Worcs. WR14 1PD
United Kingdom
Tel: 01684 561567
E-mail: allan@aspect-design.net
Website: www.aspect-design.net

A copy of this book has been deposited
with the British Library Board

Front cover photo by Robert Lloyd.
Back cover photo by Liz Dilnot Johnson.
With thanks to both.

ISBN 978-1-916919-20-4

Contents

Preface

Traumatised by his seventieth birthday, aging juvenile Stephen Chappell uses poetry to make sense of life, death, the universe, and everything. He is currently wondering where he left his car-keys.

Stephen says:

> These Poetic Outbursts are a gathering of poems I have performed at open mic's recently at Ledbury Poetry Festival's brilliant Diversions evenings (https://ledburypoetry.org.uk/) as well as at HomEnd Poets (https://www.folklife.uk/homend-poets) and Malvern Spoken Word (https://malvernspokenword.blogspot.com/).
>
> Some have been published in *Flights of the Dragonfly*, *One Hundred Poems for Hearing Dogs*, *The Nature of Hereabouts* and Winchester Poetry Festival's Railway200 project.
>
> I hope you like them – I had a lot of fun writing them!

A selection is available, illustrated and read by the author on Stephen's PoeticOutbursts YouTube channel and on his Leonardodabasildon Instagram account.

You Tube PoeticOutbursts

Leonardodabasildon

poetic.outbursts70@gmail.com

Malvern, October 2024

We've Been Sold a Pup

We've been sold a pup.
Pink bellied, soft eyed
covered with a downy hide
that peachy smell and pungent ears
we've got her now for fifteen years!

Our urgent task? Get her to ask (nicely)
when she wants to 'go'
calm her, let her sweetly show,
not always be quite so fast
when people, cats and dogs go past;
slow down a bit –
moderate that incessant
well-meant tender lick
the charging after every stick –
but ever so gently daft and fond
as we try and get her to respond:

not to bark when no-one's there
calmly walk beside,
come here!
Not imitate a mule
not turn the walk into a duel
not shred the log basket kindling
nor charge about in manic mingling

stop greeting every new stranger by jumping up.

We've delightfully been sold a lovely pup!

Puppy Says NO!

Unspeakable behaviour must be chastised
we shall not allow canine naughtiness
we must train this pup to be a good girl!

But Dog has other ideas
and Puppy says NO!

Pulling on the lead must be stopped
jumping at people must be scotched
eating poo (especially one's own)
cannot be allowed!

But Dog has other ideas
and Puppy says NO!

Goosing is gross
chasing cats makes them cross
running off and getting lost –
these are the things that must be changed
they make me mad and completely deranged!

But Dog has other ideas
and Puppy says NO!

Sulking when told off
is a mood that must be crossed off
bounding about is fine for a bit
but not all day long and one must admit

that stuffing your nose in a visitor's armpit
is behaviour that MUST be lost.

But Dog has other ideas
and Puppy says NO!

Owls are scary
cats are lairy
kids are wary
this pup is barely
able (while skulking under the table)
of obeying me quite rarely . . .

I must be strict
enforce my interdict
although sadly I'll predict

That Dog has other ideas
and Puppy says NO!

At 5.00 a.m.

At 5.00 a.m. the cat arrives, damp
from night-time showers
fresh from his wild-kill bowers.

Stealthy, he swings up past the lamp,
lands heavily on the bed,
jumps nimbly across my head,
thankfully, settles down,
gratefully, deep into a purr,
stretches, sleeps, the merest blur
on my dim dreaming.

The dog awakes, joins the cat on the bed
stretches languorously
settles down magnanimously,
lapses into a snoring slumber,
limbs jerking in a dreaming lumber
cumbering the coverlet with the heavy clog
of night-time dog.

At 6.00 a.m. an owl hoots.
the cat still drowses
but the dog of course rouses,
they are (not yet) in cahoots.

Dog has a vigorous scratch
slurping over that troublesome patch
snorts hard and attempts to combobulate,

gets me to accept my inevitable fate
and get out of bed to make
the morning pets' collation.

They are definitely in cahoots now
and to make sure I bow
to their need for me to kowtow
and serve up their chow
the cat utters a plangent meow:
a lambent salutation,
a beneficent oblation

a bed emptying displacement
and I am up and following orders.

Though still dark
the day's arc
has begun.

Dog and cat are one
and have won;
both clever arousers
and I am up and pondering:
who is wearing the trousers?

My Dog's a Secret Vegetarian

My dog's a secret vegetarian
she only eats meat on:
Mondays
Tuesdays
Wednesdays
Thursdays
Fridays
Saturdays
Sundays.

All the other days she prefers:
Puy lentils,
a slither of finely shaved truffle
drizzled with extra virgin olive oil.

She is not spoiled at all
and we love her.

Other than that she is a perfectly normal dog.

Why Do Cats?

Why do cats like cushions?
Pillows, duvets, all the cosy woollens?
Curled up by the radiator,
grinning like an alligator
on our best armchair.

They love me I'm quite sure
but

I'm beginning to believe,
and I'm willing to concede,
despite all the burnishing:
they prefer the soft furnishing.

Gorgeousness

She sleeps,
snores softly,
sprawls on the sofa
like a vast, velveteen pillow,
her downy softness enveloping
the folds of cushions and throws.

Lolling languorously,
stretched right to the edge,
spreading her four padded feet
into plain air.

Her doggy warmth
spills into
and joins the
fuggy warmth
of the warm winter room.

Her eyes flicker.
Mid-snort she wakes –
arises,
stretches,
shakes,
gazes at me
as I stand by her
booted, lead in hand.

She bounds awake now,
slides,
like jelly emerging from a mould,
into a heap
at my feet:
ready,
keen as mustard,
for the gorgeousness,
the sheer pleasure,
of the afternoon walk.

Late Afternoon Winter Dog Walking

Past the sarcastic quackering of the ducks,
arguing over connubial rights
or a piece of fish,
we go deeper into the tawny woods,
squelching through winter mud.

The dog putters off happily into the thickets,
dragging moss-crusted logs to
disembowel into soft splinters,
leaving a scattering behind us
like the lost child in the grim tales:
unspooling, unmoored,
heading for the wolf's lair
or the witch's clutches.

Luckily we know where we are.
We are not characters in some grisly tale
and end up, safely, by the soggy lake,
skirt the boggy cricket pitch,
plunge down a darkening lane
and regain the car
just as the sun sets and blazes:
winter reds, flaming umbers.

We clamber down the rutted roads home,
safe, sated, satisfied –
before dark settles and the quiet
comfortable scene becomes
a shadowed place of strange scuttlings,

where grisly tales could credibly unfold
in the impenetrable thickets,
in the shut-out cold of old, storied,
night time wild.

The Witching Hour

It is the Witching Hour
when only the Dead, Vampires
and Investment Bankers
are about.

In the cursed dark,
I stumble into Nightime's bower
dog in tow,
under a raddled moon.

It is silent,
but for the screaming
of an occasional car.
The dog pukes,

rallies,
snuffs, intent,
catches a scent,
zigzags,

pursues something
that isn't there.
Then I see the blood,
black, gleaming by moonlight,

follow the trail
reach a crushed bundle:
Badger's guts and fur.
Mystery solved.

I pull the dog away,
leave the mangled corpse,

hear a car roar past.

Proper Working Farm

The boy loves the farm dog who becomes his friend, his best friend;
they go for long, long walks every day and there is love in both their eyes.

The dog, still a pup herself, has her first litter.
As is custom, her pups are taken away.
Drowned.
There is no place for them,
they are a nuisance here on a Proper Working Farm.

The boy loves the farm dog who becomes his friend, his best friend;
they go for long, long walks every day and there is love in both their eyes.

The dog, still a pup herself, has her second litter.
As is custom, her pups are taken away.
Drowned.
There is no price to be had for them,
useless here on a Proper Working Farm.

The boy loves the farm dog who becomes his friend, his best friend;
they go for long, long walks every day and there is love in both their eyes.

The dog, still a pup herself, misses her lost ones,
bares her teeth, bites the boss.
As is custom she is put down.
There is no place for a boss biter,
a danger here on a Proper Working Farm.

The boy loved the farm dog who has gone and can no longer be his
    friend, his best friend;

they cannot go for long, long walks every day and there is no longer
love in anyone's eyes.

The boy comes home from school. The dog is gone.
'It is custom, biters must be put down' Father says
'Dry your eyes, don't be a silly fool.
We can't have dogs like that here
on a Proper Working Farm.'

The boy doesn't dry his eyes, he misses his friend, his best friend.
The boy is lonely now and the farm is a sad place, an empty place,
a Proper Working Farm.

When We're Gone

When we're gone
the canyons of Canary Wharf
will fill with birch
and sycamore thickets,
ivy will dwarf the storied towers.

Upriver the Shard will gleam with flowers,
the London parks will spill
down the Thames
making amends for all past
concrete and tarmac.

Parliament will become a bower
sweetening the quiet air,
alive with birdsong
and the bark
of deer.

The M25 will be clear
with meadowsweet grazed
by liberated cows
while sheep multiply gently up the M1,
waving thick tails and proud bums.

Forest will skirt,
take back the land
in a bland blanket
right up to John O'Groats
and far south to the bosky coasts.

Microplastics will clump
into islands,
float in a teeming sea
where weird creatures will patiently
digest our discards.

Wastelands will thrive,
hedgehogs will have
whole roads to themselves.
The planet will go its sweet way
without our drive and delve,

unrecorded, unobserved
without ourselves.

I've Fallen in Love with a Goat Called Megan

that's what she said,
causing an astonished titter
at the Dinner Table.

Turned out Megan wasn't a Goat at all,
much to our disappointment.
In her nervousness at 'coming out'
our friend, whom we'd always assumed

just hadn't found the right man,
had mangled her words somehow,
letting us know
she too was gay.

It's never easy coming out,
just like it's never easy
falling in love,
(but marvellous when you do).

A Goat? one of us said.
What? she replied
and the embarrassment
of the moment was passed.

Megan turned out to be lovely
when we finally got to meet her
and they are still together,
which says something about:
the enduring power of the Goat.

Flagging

putting out more flags and waving them,
snagging their tattered remnants on the messy rags
of past pomp or lost football games or the Proms.

Flagging down the speeding cars at the finish of some noisy metalled
    rowdy race;
or the juggernaut we face at speed, not death yet, please, give us some
    grace,
slow down, you'll get us all in the end as we go, gently, round the bend.

Flagging, equally balefully, planting your flag on someone else's plot
or, rather pointlessly, the moon, or, someday I suppose, some far distant
    spot: another planet,
when we get beyond ourselves, if we ever do.

Flagging: something a bitch does in heat, indicating with her tail she'd
    favour
a damn good rogering by any passing male,
still intact, up for it, keen to breed, wagging.

Flagging: for me not wagging, like today's effortful bagging of the
    weekly trash:
parcelling up early the bulging stash for the bin men in the littered
    streets, then limping back,
spent, sagging, for a last snatched snooze between the sheets, as too
    soon the new day dawns.

Flagging: not just lagging, for what else is a poem but flagging what I
    am and how I think

and feel, in front of startled friends, relations and, hopefully, complete,
     but paying, strangers,
keen to imbibe my spiel, pondering the scattered thoughts I deal.

Flagging: still being here to wave awhile not yet ready to snuff it
despite the whole damn boiling, reaching spill-over in the mad, bad,
     sad old world
that gives us so much to flag about.

Portrait of the Artist

There is the 'Poor Me'
whiney Me –
I am that quite a lot –
and the furious
'Don't They Realise Who I Am?' –
that Me makes me smirk.

More often though
I am 'Rueful Me',
just trying
to get through the day
without crying,
tearing hair or shouting.

I like most
'Transported Me'
when all the other *Me*s
pipe down a bit
and I gasp
at something
that has struck:

a sunset;
any form of kindness;
stillness inside an empty church;
a hill crested with trees;
the limerent touch of my dog;
a familiar arm cradling me
as the long day closes.

Early

Barely light,
gulls clatter onto rooftop perches,
settle, as dawn glimmers.
A startled chirrup strengthens
to a throaty tune-free yell,
ululating in full cliff-clung clamour:
echoing, exultant, shrieking
– AGAIN! AGAIN! AGAIN! –

Crow cries curse from guttural gullets:
– UCK! UCK! –
deep bellied overtones flung
– rude, audacious, atrocious –
across cluttered rooves
stinging the world aware
with deep-throat
bird-shit scorn.

Elsewhere:
dogs bark,
bikes scoot down concrete chasms;
a car whinnies,
starlings skitter,
sparrows chatter,
pigeon thud scatters,
a distant deer grunts,
owls' shrieks vanish.

Silence.
Swans wings swoosh,
carving a lapidary gash
through thickening air.
A blackbird sings
to the rising day-begun sun.

Swiftly,
dawning roar clambers,
drowning bird-squawk:
dredging into the ruck
of morning motion rush,
sending my shattered dawn
packing.

I Just Thought You Ought to Know . . .

it was you who made life worth living
when I was young and so longing,
you who did the loving back then,

led me alight in your eyes
like no other,
what transformations you made flow.

Now, fat with contentment,
love's rapture faded,
yet assurance remains,

being loved, wanted, valued –
all I so longed for before
and thought I'd never know,

still, here now: so better –
and I love you too
and well,

I just thought you ought to know . . .

Author Biography

Stephen Chappell was born in London in 1954 and did not start writing poetry till he was pushing seventy – a late life pleasure which has changed and delighted him in what is turning out to be a very pleasant dotage.

He is gay, Civil Partnered to Robert with whom he has spent, so far, 43 happy years. They live halfway up the Malvern hills have two cats and a gorgeous dog called Molly.

Stephen has had work published in *Flights* (Flights of the Dragonfly) and features in anthologies by Ledbury's HomEnd Poets and the Hereabouts Poets' *The Nature of Herefordshire*. A selection of his work can also be found on the website of Malvern Spoken Word (https://malvernspokenword.blogspot.com/) and on Instagram and YouTube .

He sums himself up in the poem 'Portrait of the Artist': 'There is the "Poor Me"/whiney Me –/I am that quite a lot' and is easily moved by 'any form of kindness . . . the limerent touch of my dog;/ a familiar arm cradling me/as the long day closes.'

CLINICAL PRACTICE AND THE LAW

A legal primer for clinicians

Published by Professional Solutions Publications

Giles Eyre

This edition is published in 2018 by Professional Solutions Publications, 12 Bloomsbury Square, London WC1A 2LP

Professional Solutions Publications is an imprint of: Professional Solutions Learning and Development (www.prosols.uk.com)

Typeset in Minion Pro and Lato by Karen Arnott, Graphic Designer, 14a High Street, West Wratting, Cambridge. CB21 5LU. (www.karenarnott.co.uk)

EDITORS' NOTE: The views set out in this text are those of the author alone. Whilst great care has been taken in connection with the preparation of this work, no liability whatsoever can be accepted in respect of the material contained herein by the author or publishers. The reader is directed to the legislation, case law and other primary materials referred to in the text. Medical opinion used in this book is provided only for the purpose of illustrating medico-legal principles and the authors do not put forward the medical opinions expressed as definitive of medical opinion.

ISBN 978-0-9569341-2-3

A Cataloguing-in-Publication record is available for this book from the British Library.

Author

Giles Eyre

Giles Eyre is a recently retired barrister and an Associate Member of Chambers at 9 Gough Square, London (www.9goughsquare.co.uk). Giles has extensive experience in conducting and advising in personal injury, industrial disease and clinical negligence claims. He was trained as a mediator and was appointed a Recorder in 2004.

Giles regularly presents seminars, through Professional Solutions Learning and Development and in his own right, for medical practitioners and other expert witnesses on legal principles, effective report writing and court room skills. He is co-author (with Lynden Alexander) of Writing Medico-Legal Reports in Civil Claims – an essential guide (2nd edition 2015), published by Professional Solutions Publishing (www.prosols.uk.com), and regularly writes articles on the subject. He blogs on issues relevant to court experts in civil claims – with particular but not exclusive relevance to medical experts - at www.medico-legalMinder.net.

Professional Solutions Learning and Development

Professional Solutions has been presenting workshops to expert witnesses since 1996. Its small group training workshops are targeted to the needs of the professionals attending each training session and it has established an excellent reputation for the quality of its training. The training is presented by highly experienced barristers and forensic communication consultants.

Lynden Alexander and Giles Eyre have been presenting workshops together for nearly 20 years and are knowledge leaders in the field of expert witness training. They have created a programme of seminars, practical workshops, e-learning and publications to support the learning of professionals who are seeking to achieve the highest standards of practice in expert witness work.

For further information about the workshop programme and other learning resources, please visit: www.prosols.uk.com.

Acknowledgements

I would like to thank the many people, medics and lawyers, who have been prepared to discuss this project with me and to share their views and comments. I am grateful to Lynden Alexander of Professional Solutions Learning and Development for both years of discussions on this topic but also some of the materials adapted for this book.

The earliest discussions about the need for a book such as this were with Dr Simon Tordoff. A number of doctors, including Dr Rajesh Munglani, Dr Francesca Elwen and Dr Lucie Cocker have more recently suggested topics for inclusion and to all of them I am grateful. For particular mention is Dr Adam Collins, whose suggestions and many comments on the draft helped hone this into the book it now is.

I offer particular thanks to James Badenoch QC, Chairman Emeritus of the Expert Witness Institute, and leading counsel in the landmark case of Montgomery (among many others), Michael Foy, Consultant Orthopaedic and Spinal Surgeon and Chairman of the Medico-Legal Committee of the British Orthopaedic Association, and Dr Jan Wise, Consultant Psychiatrist and Chair of the British Medical Association's Medico-Legal Committee, for taking the time to provide forewords to this text.

Any errors in the text are however the sole responsibility of the author.

Finally I thank my wife Jennet for her patience with the time I have taken up on this project.

Writing Medico-Legal Reports in Civil Claims – an Essential Guide (2nd Edition)

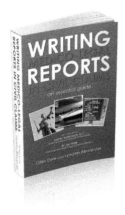

Publication: September 2015
Online price: £59.95 + £5 postage & package
at: www.prosols.uk.com

"An essential and invaluable resource for all involved in medico-legal work as expert witnesses... an invaluable aid to legal understanding and to the enhancement of the expert's practical skills." James Badenoch Q.C.

"A must-have-manual for the new expert - a go-to-guide for the mature expert." Dr Jan Wise Chair of the BMA Medico-Legal Committee 2004 -2015

Written for medical experts by Giles Eyre and Lynden Alexander and published in association with the Expert Witness Institute, this highly-praised guide to medico-legal report writing in civil claims bridges the 'communication void' that too often exists between medical experts and the lawyers who instruct them. The guide explains the legal principles and rules of court that must be applied in writing reports, gives guidance on the report's content and format, provides practical forensic writing skills, and explores the practical and contractual issues that arise in medico-legal practice.

The text includes:

- Case law and recent decisions relevant to medico-legal work
- The Civil Procedure Rules, Practice Directions and Pre-Action Protocols, and the 'Guidance for the instruction of experts in civil claims' 2014, with commentary and explanation
- Guidance on how to report effectively on:
    - Personal Injury and Clinical Negligence claims
    - Causation issues in straightforward and complex claims
    - Acceleration, exacerbation, exaggeration and malingering
    - Practical issues relating to video evidence
    - Mental capacity
    - Heads of claim, including disability in domestic and employment settings
- Quantum and Care reporting
- Guidance on the drafting of joint statements
- Extended consideration of the Bolam test and the new Montgomery consent law
- Discussion of the increasing requirement for shorter and more focussed reports and the skills needed to achieve this
- Practical issues that arise in medico-legal practice and model terms of engagement

For more information on this guide and to purchase it, please visit www.prosols.uk.com

Contents

Foreword

James Badenoch QC

Alarm and concern, and even fear and loathing, have often in my long experience characterised attitudes to the law among sections of the medical and related professions. All too often this stems from a bewildered ignorance, or partial and so faulty understanding, of how the law relates to clinical practice, and of how it works when clinicians find themselves involved with it. Understandable though this may be (and obvious gaps in professional training are at least partly to blame) such attitudes can be very harmful, given their adverse effect on the confidence and the morale of clinicians in the difficult work they do in increasingly challenging conditions.

It is that ignorance and misunderstanding which this book sets out to dispel. It does so by providing in an accessible style and format a straightforward explanation of the legal principles which apply generally, and also which apply less commonly but crucially, to clinical practice and to clinicians' experience of the legal system. As examples of its scope and importance as a working text, it covers among other things: the legal versus the scientific approach to evidence and to proof; negligence and how it is defined; the components of medical crime; the principles of patient consent and confidentiality; the duty of candour; whistleblowing; record keeping and expert witness work. There is a wealth of information and wise advice within its pages.

It is Giles Eyre's direct experience in the practice of these areas of the law, and his gift for clear and uncomplicated exposition, which makes this book so useful. It will be welcomed by lawyers in the field for their own use, but above all it vitally fills a gap for clinicians. Those in established clinical practice would do well to consult it as a matter of course, and it deserves to become a basis for study for those in training. I am delighted to welcome it and to commend it.

James Badenoch Q.C.
September 2018

Michael Foy FRCS

Consultant Orthopaedic & Spinal Surgeon

As medical practitioners we are obliged to be familiar with the law as it applies to our day to day clinical practice. Many of us also have closer, more direct links to the legal profession through our work as expert witnesses in personal injury and clinical negligence claims. Less commonly, hopefully, we have to talk to solicitors because we are the subject of a complaint or litigation in our own practice.

In our medical training, both at undergraduate and post-graduate level, our required knowledge of the law, the workings of the legal mind and the practicalities of dealing with solicitors as advocate or expert, is given very little attention. Giles Eyre seeks to address this deficiency in our education and training in this publication. Giles has extensive experience of dealing with doctors through his legal practice, his work as an educator through Professional Solutions, his lectures/seminars, his articles on medico-legal matters and his blog. He has contributed to a number of medico-legal sessions at the annual British Orthopaedic Association congress. Therefore he is ideally qualified to give advice on such matters to the medical profession.

The landscape in our own profession and the interface between the medical profession and the legal profession has moved substantially in my 30 years as a consultant in orthopaedic and spinal surgery. Thirty years ago complaints and claims against doctors were rare, now they are commonplace. National Health Service Resolution (NHSR) in their latest report show that claims against medical practitioners have increased substantially in the last thirty years (892 claims 1988/89 v 6,088 claims 2008/9 v 10,686 2017/18). NHSR estimates the money set aside for clinical negligence claims at £77 billion in 2018. This makes it the third biggest call on future Government resources after pensions and nuclear de-commissioning! Professional indemnity payments are rising exponentially for doctors. The Medical Defence Union (MDU) have stopped indemnifying spinal surgeons. The overall trends suggest that in our clinical careers we are very likely to seek advice from or give advice to solicitors.

Against this background it becomes abundantly clear that a knowledge of the law and its relationship to both clinical and expert witness practice is essential. An understanding of the way a lawyer's brain works and how he/she interprets evidence is well covered in this book. The importance of clear, concise record keeping is emphasised. The number of times that I have been asked to advise in potential negligence claims and the contemporaneous records are deficient and appalling is too many to count. It often renders a potentially defensible claim indefensible. There are useful practical guidelines on dealing with police enquiries and what to do when issues arise in one's own practice. More recent changes to the law relating to Duty of Candour and the Montgomery Ruling on consent are also discussed. Even after 30 years of involvement in medico-legal practice alongside my clinical/surgical practice I have found the book to be instructive and educational. I commend it to you.

Michael A Foy FRCS
Consultant Orthopaedic & Spinal Surgeon
September 2018

Dr M E J Wise

MSc FRCPsych IDFAPA

Most of us came into medicine to heal, or at least to comfort the afflicted. Few imagined the bureaucracy that follows, or realised how high emotions run when things go wrong, and being human they will go wrong - because systems are flawed, or because disability and death are part of that, so far inevitably, terminal condition - life. Few of us expect the acrimony and hostility that can follow, particularly when disciplinary or legal procedures follow. We are poorly served at Medical School, although the defence organisations make a valiant effort subsequently to educate those more concerned with pathology finals, college exams, or debt! Mr Eyre tackles this lacuna.

In this pocket-sized guide he covers a wide range of topics from how lawyers think and the nature of evidence and 'proof' to the increasingly important and seemingly omnipresent issues of 'when things go wrong'! He explains the lawyer's approach to records and their analysis and why the schoolmaster's adage, that you get more marks for showing the (thinking) process than the actual answer, holds as true in Court as it did for Finals!

By walking the medic though a lawyer's thought processes he helps us see how we can record our observations, the history, the reasoning, and the logic, in a way that will not only lead to better care, but less litigation – or at the very least potential litigation more quickly resolved! This book will help us understand that concern about the nature of evidence we record is not philosophical navel-gazing , but of critical importance.

In today's digital world, consent and information processing are minefields. With adept dissection the different aspects of the regulatory and statutory demands are explained. Mr Eyre illustrates why recording what happened is paramount; and this provides the rationale for taking as long as it takes to carry out that task to the required standard.

This work explains how the current chilly climate around doctors' performance increases the need to deliver proper care that is neither rushed nor slap-dash, and which includes recording the evidence properly. With huge demands on practitioners with a never-ending workload, the temptation to do only the most urgent tasks will inevitably lead to problems. Understanding how the evidence is weighed helps justify why tasks must not be short-changed on time, and explains why it is better not to do a new task than leave it incompletely done or incompletely recorded.

The chapter 'When things go wrong', whilst hopefully unnecessary for most, provides a focus on why the earlier lessons should be adhered to, as well as the need to practise within available resources and competencies. The comprehensive explanation of the ways in which legal processes can interfere when things do go wrong should not induce panic attacks, but caution, not avoidance but engagement and further reflection on ways to ensure medical records provide adequate evidence of the thought processes and reasoning behind the decisions when viewed retrospectively.

This introductory guide provides information of importance for those anxious about the boundaries between medical practice and the law, and who wish to equip themselves better for a career in medicine in which field the law increasingly exercises oversight.

Dr M E J Wise
MSc FRCPsych IDFAPA
September 2018

Author's note

This book was initially conceived of as being a guide for junior doctors. It does this by doing 3 things.

Firstly it explains, so far as it impacts on the clinician's life, how a lawyer's mind works – the lawyer's approach to investigating events, how a lawyer decides what weight any particular evidence carries and why, how evidence should be presented to any third party and the difference between factual and expert evidence.

Secondly the book explains in simple terms the law as it impacts on issues and events a doctor is likely commonly to experience, including confidentiality, capacity and consent, and interactions with the police, and helps the doctor to prepare for them and to record relevant observations, actions and decisions for future reference, whether by other clinicians or in court.

Thirdly it seeks to take some of the fear out of what happens 'when things go wrong' by explaining the different proceedings and inquiries which may result from an unexpected death, a serious complaint, or an accusation of negligence, and the legal framework in which they operate, and which will all be far less troubling if the lessons given earlier in the book have been put into practice.

After 40 years working professionally with clinicians from many specialities and of varied experience, I have no doubt that their professional lives would have been easier if they had started with the knowledge that this book would have given them (if it had been written then); they would have been better prepared, they would have worried less, they would have been better witnesses, whether witnesses of fact or expert witnesses, and whether on behalf of themselves or on behalf of others, and they would have left a much clearer and more comprehensible trail of notes and records for others to interpret than the countless thousands of entries I have spent a career trawling through, trying to interpret and understand. Therefore there is much in this book that the senior colleagues of the junior doctors would benefit from even at this stage of their careers.

The choice of topics the book covers is mine. There is much that I have not included, because the law interferes in nearly everything, but the aim was to focus on the key topics, which will also help illustrate the general principles, and to keep the book to a manageable size, and provide some important answers and important skills. If you think there is something the next edition should include, let me know – I too am happy to learn!

Giles Eyre
September 2018
London

1

Introduction

Medicine and the law

All healthcare professionals operate within a legal context in much the same way that all lawyers live within a medical context and probably with a similar degree of understanding (or misunderstanding) of the relevant principles. The lack of understanding creates unnecessary fears and itself results in further misunderstanding. As a consequence, the clinician's daily practice does not have the benefit of being informed by those unknown or misunderstood principles, and this frequently causes unnecessary worry and concern and creates unnecessary difficulties or complications at a later date when that practice is subject to further consideration or criticism.

At a time when complaints to the GMC and other professional regulatory bodies are running at an all-time high, when NHS hospitals display advertising for lawyers advising on clinical negligence claims on which the NHS is paying out over a billion pounds a year in damages, when insurance and professional indemnity rates are soaring, and when clinicians find themselves being investigated for possible prosecution for gross negligence manslaughter, it could not be more important for clinicians of all kinds to understand how the law impacts on their practice and how they can best protect themselves from being on the wrong end of a claim or complaint.

This guide will look at the main legal principles relevant to a clinician's practice:-

- how lawyers and judges address evidence and proof and why that matters to the clinician;
- the court and tribunal system, the bewildering maze of possible forums in which a clinician might appear;
- how to draft, or help draft, a witness statement;
- the requirements for establishing complaints, prosecutions and claims against clinicians, and investigating their actions and the consequences of them;
- how the law effects clinical practice when consenting and communicating with patients, dealing with adverse events and apologising,
- making decisions in relation to those unable to make decisions themselves;
- the rules about detaining patients requiring emergency treatment;
- the clinician's position in a police inquiry, and issues of patient confidentiality both in relation to alleged crime and generally;

Throughout, this book will demonstrate the importance of keeping full, clear, concise and readily comprehensible records of clinical actions and decisions in order to provide a contemporaneous explanation available to throw light on past actions when they call to be revisited, and shows how best to do so. It will also help the clinician who has to communicate with a lawyer to understand the approach of a lawyer and the nature of the information most required.

We will also take a brief look at providing expert evidence for court or other hearings.

In addressing the clinician and the substantive law, this book is not intended to be the last word but rather to be an introduction to the law and to act as a practical guide to the main principles and to other sources of useful information which will assist the clinician.

This book addresses the law in England and Wales, the law in which the author was trained and under which he practised throughout his career. It does not address the law outside that jurisdiction in which the author is not qualified including the laws of Scotland or Northern Ireland. While the general principles are what a lawyer would call 'common sense', and in some subjects covered by this book there are similarities throughout England, Wales, Scotland and Northern Ireland, readers will have to look for guidance elsewhere if concerned specifically with the law as it is in Scotland or Northern Ireland.

2

A lawyer's mind

Chapter outline

This Chapter will give a greater understanding of the way that a lawyer approaches facts and evidence. With the benefit of this understanding, clinicians will improve descriptions of their actions and the reasoning behind their decisions, and avoid ambiguity, which will help inform those coming after them, whether in a clinical setting or when their work is put under a critical spotlight. These descriptions may be in contemporaneous records and notes or in subsequent spoken or written evidence.

A lawyer's training affects how the lawyer interprets words, and therefore there is importance for the lawyer in how words are used, and which words are used, whether spoken or written.

This Chapter will also describe how complex medical matters can be explained to those uninitiated into the ways of the clinician, such as lawyers. This will both inform that audience as to those matters and also enable them to approach the complex issues facing clinicians in a critical manner, and so be able better to compare and weigh up different opinions on the same issues.

Lawyers, and hence judges, give different weight to different evidence. There is greater weight in showing the reasoning process behind a decision, as also in contemporaneous documentary evidence over a subsequent spoken account, and consistency between accounts of past events is key to the credibility of evidence.

2.1   Use of words

For lawyers, words really matter. This is equally true when lawyers are considering or investigating the actions or inactions of experts other than lawyers as when dealing with other lawyers. For a lawyer there is the world of difference between saying something 'possibly happened' and 'probably happened', or 'could' or 'would' or 'should' have happened, or 'might', 'may', 'can', 'will' or 'shall' happen. Similarly to say a patient was 'better' begs the question whether the patient was cured or simply less unwell; to say symptoms have 'reduced' or 'improved' says nothing about what the current situation is or how that compares with the unreduced or unimproved situation. These differences in the use of language matter to a lawyer, and therefore will matter to any clinician involved, because they may make the difference between winning or losing a case, or in establishing whether a clinician was in breach of duty or of professional standards or of the law, or how much is recovered by way of damages in a claim arising out of an accident or out of clinical negligence.

> USE WORDS CLEARLY AND AVOID AMBIGUITY,
> BOTH WHEN SPEAKING AND WRITING

This is not because the lawyer is a pedant – although some may be – but because the lawyer requires precision, and particularly in evidence which is to be used in court or for other legal processes, and language is the medium through which such precision must be provided. Conversely the lawyer looks for a lack of clarity or a degree of uncertainty in order to weaken or undermine the opposing side's case, and the evidence and opinion that purports to support it, and such imprecision or ambiguity may well provide such material. Similarly, any apparent inconsistency in the evidence provided on different occasions or from different sources, even if not noticed by the clinician, will be used by a lawyer to raise doubts about the quality and reliability of the evidence.

It is essential therefore for the clinician to learn to be precise when speaking or writing. Clinical records, witness statements, oral evidence and expert reports may all prove ambiguous or unhelpful, or even unintentionally damaging, because of such inaccuracies or imprecision. Accuracy and precision through the careful use of language is required to provide a proper account of one's thoughts and actions when called to account for them.

2.2 Logic

Doctors when presented with a patient use their training and previous experience to look for patterns of symptoms and signs, may make some investigations, and come to a diagnosis. It is a natural and everyday part of the work for which they have been trained. In the same way it may seem obvious to a clinician that a certain treatment will usually have certain effects. For example:-

> *The administration of a diuretic will cause blood pressure to drop through the mechanism of production of a diuresis, that is an increased production of urine.*

Or:

> *A lack of oxygen to an anesthetised and ventilated patient will cause the blood to darken and the patient to appear blue.*

However, lawyers do not have (or cannot be assumed to have) any implicit medical knowledge and yet they need to understand in basic terms how one thing in medicine leads to another and the working of the medical mind. In other words, without medical knowledge or training the lawyer has to be able to understand the principle at work and the chain of events giving rise to, or which might explain, the identified outcome.

The lawyer needs the clinician to explain in simple, clear, concise and logical terms what is happening. For the examples given above, more useful explanations for a lawyer would be that:-

> *Heart failure can cause additional fluid to build up in the blood vessels and tissues, causing swelling of the limbs or respiratory failure. The administration of a diuretic will cause blood pressure to drop because the drug causes the kidneys to increase the amount of salt and water that is excreted as urine. The resulting reduction in volume of fluid will reduce swelling and improve respiratory function, but will also reduce blood pressure. Some diuretics also cause the walls of the blood vessels to relax and widen, making it easier for blood to flow through, and again lowering blood pressure.*

Or that:-

> *A lack of oxygen to an anesthetised and ventilated patient will cause the blood to darken through the mechanism of hypoxaemia, that is an abnormally low concentration of oxygen in the blood, which results in the deoxygenation of haemoglobin, which then becomes darker in colour and gives the patient the appearance of being blue.*

This need to explain is even greater where (as is common in medicine) there are several possible explanations, or factors which may be relevant. For example, the question may arise as to why a patient had a low blood pressure post-operatively.

This requires the doctor to identify all of the possible causes and to explain which of the causes is most likely and why. The low blood pressure may be due to the residual effects of the anaesthetic, overdose of other drugs, lack of fluids, lack of steroids, lack of oxygen, heart failure, too much analgesia, sepsis or unrecognized bleeding. The lawyer needs to understand how a clinician reasons in assessing the likely differential diagnosis, eliminating some less likely explanations, and rating others with different levels of likelihood, and then arrives at a clinical decision from which a particular course of treatment can be decided on, and why one course of action is preferable or more logical than another.

The lawyer asks of the clinician that those fact(or)s which are considered material (readings, observations etc) are identified. Then the reasoning based on those fact(or)s, which helps form a differential diagnosis and the possible alternative clinical treatments, should be described and explained. Finally the relative likelihood of each potential diagnosis and the implications of each potential course of action is explained, resulting in the explanation of the preferred or alternative treatment options. In that way the lawyer can quickly understand the logic of the clinician's account and how the conclusion flows from the available facts, and is also able to test the propositions relied on. Without having the doctor's expertise, the lawyer can follow the clinical principles at work and the working of the clinician's mind and weigh that up against any other alternative medical opinion that may be expressed on similar information. The lawyer can also understand the importance of establishing the factual matrix – the framework of facts - on which the reasoning is based and assess the issues relevant to proving those facts.

The clinical records, although of course they need to be concise and will need to be completed speedily in most cases, should try to reflect this practice. The notes should identify the material facts, any differential diagnosis and the reason for preferring one diagnosis, and with practice that can be done concisely and quickly.

Whether dealing with an oral account or witness statement, or looking at contemporaneous clinical records, the lawyer should be able to identify the logic of what has taken place. Leaving out the identification of material fact(or)s and the reasoning process when making clinical records not only does not help the lawyer but, as we will see, can create very real difficulties for the clinician when asked to justify a diagnosis or treatment option many months later, or when that diagnosis or treatment option comes under close scrutiny, for whatever reason.

> IN MAKING AND RECORDING A CLINICAL DECISION, DEMONSTRATE A LOGIAL APPROACH. IDENTIFY THE MATERIAL FACTS RELIED ON, THE REASONING PROCESS BASED ON THEM AND THE WEIGHING OF ALTERNATIVES

2.3   Reasoning process

If follows from the lawyer's approach to logic, that what the lawyer needs to know from any person with expertise in another field is how that person's conclusion, based on that expertise, is reached. The process requires:

1. identification of the evidence or facts which are material to the issue being addressed, and

2. a description of the reasoning process which results in the conclusion reached.

Once this is provided, without training or experience in the area of expertise, the lawyer can assess the value of the conclusion (or opinion or decision or diagnosis) and compare it and its strength with the conclusion (or opinion or decision or diagnosis) of any other person with similar expertise on that or a similar issue. The exercise of testing such a conclusion requires the answering of two questions:

1. Has the same evidence, or facts, been identified as material (and if not, why not)?

2. Is the process of reasoning the same, and if not, why not?

This is equally relevant and applicable whether considering a clinician's diagnosis, a treatment decision, an oral explanation or the written opinion of an expert witness. In Chapter 8 below we will see how this impacts on clinical records and note-making.

> EXPLAIN DECISION MAKING
> SHOW YOUR REASONING

2.4   Oral and documentary evidence

Any consideration of the actions or inactions of a person, or of a decision made by them, requires a lawyer to start by identifying the evidence available and weighing that evidence up. We will discuss the nature and types of evidence in greater detail in Chapter 3 below, but in understanding the lawyer's mind it is important to keep in mind the distinction between an oral (spoken) account of something which has happened and a contemporaneous (or near contemporaneous) written record. With the best of intention, memory is fickle, often selective, weighted by cognitive bias and often lacking in detail, but it is also subject to innocent re-interpretation in the light of subsequent knowledge or facts. And of course it may be adapted, intentionally or unintentionally, in order to excuse past actions or inaction. In contrast, a written record, although it may be falsified, if genuinely made contemporaneously to the events to which it relates, reduces the chances of all of these failings.

This means that a careful, full and explanatory record made at the time of the events to which it relates (or made very shortly afterwards) is likely to carry greater weight when seeking to ascertain what happened and why, than an oral account given subsequently when the events are being put under a critical microscope in court or some other hearing or process.

The oral account of a person who is subsequently being criticised, or of a close friend, colleague or relation of such a person will carry less weight than the oral account of a person who happened to be present and who has no interest in the outcome of any investigation into the facts. The oral account by a doctor who is being criticised, of a patient examination carried out months before will carry less weight than that of the chaperone who was present, which in turn will carry less weight than the patient's priest who accompanied the patient to offer transport and moral support, and for whom the examination was a new experience.

> CONTEMPORANEOUS DOCUMENTARY EVIDENCE
> (IN CLINICAL RECORDS) CARRIES WEIGHT IN ANY
> SUBSEQUENT INVESTIGATION

The lawyer therefore looks for contemporaneous documentary evidence to support the oral account of a person whose actions are being criticised, and seeks to demonstrate consistency in the evidence, and failing that, looks for independent oral evidence.

2.5   Consistency and inconsistency

The last sentence above is an example of the lawyer's search for consistency. Where an oral account is consistent with the written records, that generally strengthens the weight to be attached to the oral account. If two oral accounts from different, and hopefully independent, sources are consistent, that strengthens the weight to be attached to the oral accounts.

The converse is also true. A lawyer will look for inconsistency in the evidence to raise doubts as to its reliability. Therefore, if the oral account is inconsistent in one or more respects with the documentary record, even if not in relation to a key matter, this raises a question which might point to unreliability on the part of the oral account – or occasionally the documentary record. If the oral accounts of 2 witnesses are inconsistent in some one or more respects, then that may raise doubts as to the reliability of one or other of those accounts. If the accounts given by one witness differ, for example between a written witness statement and oral testimony, or between two written accounts which have been given by that same witness, such as between a statement for a hospital serious untoward injury investigation and a subsequent witness statement in court proceedings, then that inconsistency may well be relied upon to question the reliability of one or other or both of the statements, and even to support the acceptance of an alternative account.

INCONSISTENCY IN EVIDENCE DAMAGES
CREDIBILITY

2.6   An example

In *Hassell v Hillingdon Hospitals NHS Foundation Trust*[1] the judge had to decide
whether the surgeon had given the patient a warning of possible cord injury in
consenting her for spinal surgery and the possibility of alternative treatments.
(For more about consent see Chapter 13 below.)   Having heard the evidence
of both the surgeon and the patient the judge decided, on the balance of prob-
abilities[2], that the warning was not given and alternative treatments were not
discussed.   He relied on 7 reasons for coming to that conclusion, which are worth
quoting in full as an insight into the way a judge's mind works in establishing
probable (and therefore proved) facts:

> *First although Mr Ridgeway [the surgeon] gave evidence that he had dis-
> cussed conservative treatment options including physiotherapy with Mrs
> Hassell [the patient] he accepted that he understood that Mrs Hassell had
> already had physiotherapy for her neck. Although this misunderstanding was
> understandable because Mrs Hassell had been having physiotherapy for other
> complaints, he could not have had this misunderstanding if he had discussed
> other treatment options with Mrs Hassell. This is because his misunderstand-
> ing would have been corrected by Mrs Hassell who was articulate and would
> have pointed out that she had not had physiotherapy. [The case of] Mont-
> gomery[3] makes it clear that there must be a dialogue and if there had been a
> dialogue Mr Ridgeway would have known that Mrs Hassell had not yet had
> physiotherapy for the neck and upper arm problems.*

> *Secondly it was apparent that, whatever Mr Ridgeway's strengths as a surgeon
> when carrying out the operation [his standard of care in the surgery was not
> criticised by the judge], Mr Ridgeway was not a good communicator about
> the risks of operations. I make this finding because when he gave evidence in
> chief about the risks of the operation he did not include DVT or PE which he
> had said in his witness statement he would have mentioned (and which he
> mentioned for the lower back operation in 2009 as evidenced in his letter).
> Mr Ridgeway said it was his invariable practice to mention these risks for
> the cervical discectomy and there was no obvious reason why he should have
> failed to do so, other than that his belief about his invariable practice and
> what he said sometimes differed. Even making proper allowances for the fact
> that Mr Ridgeway was in the witness box and not talking to a patient it was
> plain that his belief about what he would invariably have said was not reli-
> able. I also note that Mr Ridgeway did not identify in any of the earlier cor-*

---

1   [2018] EWHC 164, http://www.bailii.org/ew/cases/EWHC/QB/2018/164.html

2   The standard of proof is considered in Chapter 4 below

3   See Chapter 13 'Consenting' below

respondence after the operation that the letter dated 1 July 2011 contained an omission about the risks of paralysis, even though he said he had mentioned these when talking to Mrs Hassell. The fact that Mr Ridgeway's communication skills did not match his skills in the mechanics of surgery (as I have found them to be) is also evidenced by his operation note "Discectomy – ¾ through" which was not a good description of the fact that he was ¾ way through releasing the annulus from the front of C5 and C6 and not ¾ way through removing the disc. It also appears from his failure to pick up and correct the comment in the Chief Executive's letter that Mr Ridgeway was removing the protruding disc material with diathermy.

Thirdly Mrs Hassell gave clear evidence that she had not been warned about the risk of paralysis and that she would have been very concerned about that as the mother of 3 children in full-time work as head of year. I accept that studies show that many patients will not accurately remember the risks of an operation as they are explained to them, and all Judges have seen and heard honest witnesses fail to recall accurately and reliably conversations and events. However Mrs Hassell did have a particular recollection of a hoarse voice because it was relevant to her work (when she was required to shout across the playground on occasions) and asked questions about that risk. She wrote a letter complaining that she had not been told about the risk of paralysis. I consider it more likely than not, and find, that she would have had a particular recollection about paralysis if it had been mentioned to her and asked further questions if it had been mentioned.

Fourthly Mr Ridgeway said in the letter dated 26 April 2012 that the operation could result in paralysis and said "similar to risks explained with previous spinal surgery". However Mr Ridgeway's letter about risks for the lower back surgery did not mention paralysis, and he did not suggest that that letter had omitted information. If Mr Ridgeway had explained the risks to Mrs Hassell as he had for the lower back (as he said he had in his letter dated 26 April 2012) he would have failed to mention paralysis.

Fifthly Mr Ridgeway's evidence about whether he had mentioned the possibility of further injections as an alternative treatment differed between his witness statement, where it was not mentioned, and his oral evidence, where it was mentioned. This gave me no confidence in the reliability of Mr Ridgeway's recollections about what he had discussed with Mrs Hassell and when. Although the letter dated 28 July 2011 referred to a discussion about alternative treatments, this could not have been a discussion about physiotherapy for the reasons given above and must have referred to the alternative treatment options being fusion or disc replacement.

Sixthly the [surgeon's] website did not contain information allowing Mrs Hassell to understand fully the risks and benefits of the planned procedure. It is clear that the website referred back to discussions with the surgeon. However if as Mr Ridgeway said, he referred patients to his website so that they may fully understand the risks and benefits of the planned procedure (paragraph 7 *of his witness statement) it is unfortunate that crucial information about the risk of paralysis was missing.*

Seventhly the risk of spinal cord injury and paralysis was not referred to in the letter dated 28 June 2011 in circumstances where the letter was dictated in front of Mrs Hassell to ensure that she would know the risks which she was running. I accept that in the text there is reference to 1 in 1000 figure which the experts agree would be a reference to the risk of paralysis, but there is no mention of paralysis. This meant that: Mr Ridgeway did not mention paralysis to Mrs Hassell; or Mr Ridgeway did mention it and the dictating machine did not pick up the reference; or Mr Ridgeway did mention it and record it but the typist of the letter simply failed to type it. I find that there was no reference to the risk of paralysis in the letter because Mr Ridgeway did not give Mrs Hassell an explanation about the risk of paralysis. The figure of 1 in 1000 must have been mentioned at the end of the conversation but without any discussion about paralysis. This accords with the fact that Mr Ridgeway's explanations about risks were not clear or consistent, as appears above.

There can be no doubt from this judgment the importance of accuracy in giving evidence and in any underlying documents relied upon in evidence, and of consistency between oral and other evidence, and of being able to communicate well, both in this case to the patient and to the court.

> ## EVIDENCE MUST BE ACCURATE, CONSISTENT AND UNDERSTOOD

To summarise the points made in the judgment for preferring the patient's evidence over the surgeon's on the question of what was discussed:

- the surgeon showed a misunderstanding about the patient's history which was inconsistent with having had a proper discussion about treatment options
- the surgeon was 'not a good communicator' about operation risks because in oral evidence he omitted 2 risks which in his witness statement he said he would have mentioned, and yet claimed it was his 'invariable practice' to mention them
- the patient's recollection was clear and carried weight - recalling discussion about a less serious risk but not the more serious risk, and confirming that in a letter of complaint
- the surgeon asserted that in an earlier letter he warned of similar risks in previous surgery to the same patient, but that earlier letter said nothing of paralysis
- the surgeon's evidence was unreliable (about advising of alternative treatment) where his oral evidence on this differed from his witness statement which was before the court
- the surgeon asserted he referred patients to his website to understand risks and benefits, and the website omitted reference to paralysis

- the risk of paralysis was not referred to in a letter dictated in front of the patient.

The judge's analysis of the evidence demonstrates many of the issues indicated above and enabled him to come to a conclusion as to which evidence to prefer. Predominantly the decision was based on inconsistencies (or what appeared to the judge to be inconsistencies) in the surgeon's evidence.

3

Evidence

Chapter outline

In the previous Chapter we saw how fundamental to any inquiry is the quality of the evidence available, and how lawyers may regard evidence differently, and so give different weight to different evidence. In this Chapter we will consider the different kinds or categories of evidence as seen by a lawyer. This again may impact on the weight given to that evidence when it comes to be scrutinised and therefore it is important for the clinician to appreciate what category of evidence is likely to be considered most reliable. Hearsay evidence is compared with direct evidence of a fact; documentary evidence is compared with oral (spoken) evidence; while in most processes evidence is now given in prepared witness statements.

The law sees factual evidence in a very different way to expert evidence, and this Chapter will explain the difference between them.

Any perceived bias in a witness, whether a witness of fact or an expert witness, will be a basis for reducing the weight attached to that evidence, and this Chapter will consider the common categories of bias.

3.1 Factual evidence

Generally, any evidence of facts that are relevant to an issue that the court or tribunal or inquiry is to address will be admissible. That means that the evidence will be read or heard, can be commented on and will be considered by the decision maker(s) in that process. Some processes and hearings have stricter rules than others about what evidence can be put before them, but the old rule that the evidence before a court must be the best evidence of that fact is no longer generally applied.

(i) Direct evidence

Direct evidence is the evidence of a witness of facts of which they have direct knowledge, that is of something which they have directly experienced themselves with one of their senses. For example, a witness gives direct evidence of something that they saw, heard, felt or, less commonly, smelt or tasted.

(ii) Hearsay

Hearsay is the evidence of a witness of what they have been told by someone else ('first hand hearsay') or even what they have been told by someone else which that other person was told by a third person ('second-hand hearsay'). The fact that the witness was spoken to by that person is direct evidence of having had a conversation – 'I had a conversation with X'. The recollection of what the witness was told by that person is hearsay – 'X told me that the patient was not responsive at 10 am' (first hand hearsay) or 'X told me that Y told her that the patient was not responsive at 10 am' (second-hand hearsay).

By its nature hearsay evidence from a witness of what someone said is less reliable and more difficult of testing than direct evidence from that person of what they are now reported to have said, and second-hand hearsay is less reliable and more difficult to test than first hand hearsay. For that reason, in most proceedings hearsay evidence will be identified and, if it is admitted as part of the evidence in those proceedings, it will be treated with greater care than direct evidence unless the hearsay evidence is not in fact disputed. In criminal cases there is still a presumption that hearsay evidence that is not agreed will not be admitted save in exceptional circumstances because of its potential for being unreliable. In civil claims there are procedures to seek to require the original maker of the statement to attend to be cross-examined, and the care that must be taken with such evidence is set out in legislation. An inquiry or tribunal hearing may take a more relaxed approach. The more important the hearsay evidence is in the context of the dispute, and the more potentially determinant of the issue in the dispute, the greater the care that will be taken in testing it and its reliability.

As a consequence, on important factual issues a party will seek to obtain direct evidence rather than rely on hearsay, or a party challenging hearsay evidence will seek to emphasise all matters which make the recollection of the other person's statement, and the account given by that other person, less reliable, such as any potential motive for fabrication or circumstances that might result in unreliability on the part of the person giving (and recalling) the hearsay or the person who made the hearsay statement being relied upon.

Nevertheless, in some tribunals and in coroners' courts there are few constraints in using hearsay evidence and even little recognition that that is in fact the nature of the evidence.

> RECOGNISE HEARSAY EVIDENCE AND CONSIDER
> ITS LIMITATIONS

There are interesting exceptions to the 'hearsay rule' under which evidence which might at first appearance appear to be hearsay is nonetheless admissible. These are considered principally in criminal cases and include concepts such as dying declarations and *res gestae*[1], and are outside the scope of this book.

(iii)   Oral evidence

Courts used to be largely confined to having evidence proved by oral evidence. Exceptions evolved over time for convenience and practicalities (for example in relation to various public records). The giving of oral evidence is now principally limited to evidence which is controversial in the context of the issues that are to be resolved. In cases in court the witness statements of all relevant witnesses of fact will be served ahead of the case being heard, with certain exceptions principally in criminal cases where the defence do not have to serve such statements. To the extent that there is no issue with the content of such witness statements they will be agreed and admitted into evidence as written statements, or the parties may agree admissions that will bind them, and the judge, tribunal or jury, based on agreed matters within such statements.

It is of course only the oral evidence of a witness that can be tested by cross examination at a hearing.

(iv)   Witness statements

Witness statements have already been referred to above in a number of contexts. The format for witness statements to be usable in different courts and tribunals are generally laid down, the principal requirement being to ensure that the maker of such a statement prepared for such purposes is aware of the importance of telling the truth and of the possible consequences of lying, which may include imprisonment. Only witness statements with the appropriate declaration can

---

1   *Res gestae* refers to a second-hand statement by a witness which because it was made spontaneously and concurrently with an event is considered reliable.

then be relied upon in such proceedings to stand in place of the oral evidence of the witness.

In a number of circumstances a witness statement will be admissible in proceedings in the absence of agreement from the opposing party, for example if the maker has disappeared or is too ill to give evidence.

Witness statements will also be prepared other than for use in such court or tribunal proceedings, for example in order to ascertain what happened in respect of a serious incident investigation, or to inform some investigative process or a lawyer outside of, or in preparation for, proceedings. These therefore have no set format and are most unlikely to have the consequences of imprisonment should they subsequently prove to be false. However, they may still be used in proceedings to show inconsistency between different accounts given by a witness (see above).

Preparing witness statements is considered below in Chapter 6.

(v)   Documentary evidence

Documentary evidence comes in many different kinds. Contemporary records maintained in the course of treatment or monitoring of patients are perhaps the most obvious. The rules with regard to the use of such evidence in legal proceedings vary depending on the nature of the proceedings. Criminal proceedings take the most care in imposing rules to ensure the reliability of such evidence before it can be used, tribunals and inquiries the least, and civil courts come somewhere in the middle.

What someone has written or recorded on a previous occasion is always admissible in evidence against its maker to show inconsistency between that document and what has been said on later occasions or is now being said. (See Section 2.5 above for the importance of inconsistency in the legal system.) Such an earlier statement is less convincing when used by the maker of the statement as evidence of her own consistency – a 'self-serving' statement – as it is capable of being produced expressly for that purpose. This is particularly so in criminal cases, although such a statement may still be used to rebut a suggestion that the current evidence is a recent fabrication (because the current evidence is consistent with that which was given at a much earlier occasion and therefore unlikely to be fabricated). In civil proceedings, as in disciplinary proceedings, referring back to clinical records or notes, particularly those setting out clearly what was done or said, or showing the reasons for action or inaction, can be convincing evidence.

More formal documents prepared by government agencies or as business records are generally admissible without difficulty.

In a civil case all relevant documents (including clinical records) will be disclosed by one party to the other and contained in the court bundles – the copy documents produced for use at the trial – and it is provided that these should if possible be agreed to be treated as evidence of the facts stated in them[2].

3.2   Expert evidence

A witness may not give evidence of opinion on a matter unless the witness has first established an expertise which validates that opinion and the court or tribunal has consented to expert evidence being given. Otherwise the witness's evidence must be limited to matters of a factual nature.

Expert witnesses are used in order to give evidence based on their expertise, to explain relevant matters for which their expertise is needed and to express opinions based on (and within) their expertise. The expert witness therefore helps the court (or jury or tribunal) to decide issues that are beyond its (or their) technical knowledge or expertise. An expert has an overriding duty to a court (or tribunal) to be independent and objective and to assist the court (or tribunal) with matters within the expert's expertise.

Expert evidence is considered further in Chapter 7 below.

> ONLY AN EXPERT WITNESS CAN GIVE EVIDENCE OF
> OPINION

3.3   Bias

Bias will undermine the evidence of any witness, factual or expert, as it provides a motive for dishonesty or an explanation for a less than objective view. Any suspicion of bias is likely to undermine a witness's evidence and raise questions as to the objectivity of such evidence.

Bias arises in a number of different ways.

The most obvious form of bias is towards a party to a dispute. This is the clearest evidence of lack of independence. Therefore, a witness should reveal at the earliest opportunity any connection with a party to the litigation or other process (the claimant or defendant, the complainant or some other person whose actions are being investigated) or any potential conflict of interest. For example a clinician who is a witness in proceedings would be expected to set out details of having worked with or under another clinician who is a party to, or is intimately involved in, the litigation.

Bias can also arise in subtler ways. Hindsight bias can arise where an expert is asked to express an opinion on past events with an unfortunate outcome. Studies have shown that knowledge of an adverse outcome in a case affects the opinions given by medical experts as to the appropriateness of clinical treatment.

---

2   Practice direction 39A to the Civil Procedure Rules para 3.9(2)

Having knowledge of a poor outcome may, for example, cause an expert to mini-mise the management dilemmas facing the doctor at the time and to overlook the uncertainties inherent in diagnosis and treatment. A cognitive bias may arise simply on the basis of the side in a dispute instructing a witness or an expert and the expectation that arises from that.

4

Proof

Chapter outline

The question of proof arises in 2 ways: who has to prove something where its proof is in issue, and to what standard does this have to be proved to satisfy the court, tribunal or other process.

Whereas a scientific mind will most probably require at least 95% probability to regard something as 'proved', this Chapter will see how in most contexts outside criminal proceedings a court, tribunal or other process will be satisfied of something if it is established as being more likely than not, a standard which will not come naturally to the clinician.

4.1   The burden of proof

Generally speaking the person bringing a claim has to prove it. In a criminal case, it is the prosecution that has to prove that the defendant has committed a crime; in a civil case (generally a claim for damages) it is the claimant, the person seeking to recover damages, who has to prove that the defendant is in breach of duty to him and the damages which should be recovered; in a family case, it is the party asserting a fact who has to prove it; in regulatory and disciplinary proceedings, it is the professional body questioning the fitness to practise of someone that has to prove the unfitness and the need for a sanction. If that onus is not discharged then in a criminal case the defendant will be acquitted, in a civil case no damages will be awarded and in a family or regulatory matter there will be no material finding.

4.2 The standard of proof

The burden of proof is discharged to a different standard depending on the nature of the proceedings. This has recently been restated in the following manner[1]:

> As a general rule, the standard to which a putative state of affairs must be proved before it may be found as a fact by a court or tribunal depends not on the nature of the putative fact but on the nature of the proceedings. Thus, in criminal proceedings the prosecution must prove the charge beyond reasonable doubt. But in civil proceedings a lower standard of proof (on the balance of probabilities) applies. It is clearly established that this is the applicable standard in civil proceedings even in relation to an allegation of criminal conduct.

> The underlying reason why a particularly high standard of proof is required in criminal proceedings is that a criminal conviction has serious consequences for the accused, which may include loss of liberty. For that reason the standard of proof is weighted in favour of the accused to reflect the policy that it is better to let the crime of a guilty person go unpunished than to condemn an innocent person. In civil proceedings, which are generally concerned with determining the rights of parties as between each other, there is no equivalent policy reason for weighting the fact-finding exercise in favour of or against one or other party. Instead, in order to cater for those cases in which the evidence is inadequate to enable any positive finding to be made, it is sufficient and expedient simply to have a rule which requires the party who advances a case to prove that the facts relied on to support it are more likely than not to be true.

> Of course, decisions in civil proceedings can also have serious consequences for parties involved. For example, a finding in a family court of sexual abuse by a father may result in children being taken into care and could lead to a criminal prosecution being brought against the father, quite apart from causing devastating reputational damage. A large award of damages may cause a defendant financial ruin. An injunction may impose an onerous restriction on a person's freedom of action. An order for possession may result in a

---

1   *R v Kelly Shakespeare and others* [2018] EWHC 1955 at para 27, http://www.bailii.org/ew/cases/EWHC/Admin/2018/1955.html

family losing their home. Such consequences may by any practical measure be much more serious for the party affected than, say, a criminal conviction for a minor road traffic offence. The common law, however, has rejected an approach of applying a variable standard of proof. Instead, in the interests of simplicity, consistency and uniformity, a single standard of proof is applied in all civil cases, just as a single (though higher) standard of proof is applied in all criminal cases. The only exceptions are proceedings, such as proceedings for committal for contempt of court, which, although classified as civil, are functionally equivalent to criminal proceedings having regard to the possibility that a person may be sent to prison.

(i)   Criminal proceedings

Criminal proceedings are normally between the state (the Crown) and an individual, and are brought by the Crown Prosecution Service, although there are a number of other bodies who also bring criminal proceedings (such as the Health & Safety Executive, the Department of Work and Pensions, the Environment Agency, the Food Standards Agency, the Gambling Commission, the Serious Fraud Office and the RSPCA). In criminal proceedings the defendant's guilt has to be proved so that the magistrates or jury are satisfied so that they are sure of guilt before they can convict. The traditional way of expressing this was to say that they had to be sure 'beyond reasonable doubt' but the expression 'sure' is now used instead. This is never expressed in terms of a percentage.

> IN A CRIMINAL CASE, PROOF MUST BE 'BEYOND REASONABLE DOUBT' SO THAT THE FACT FINDER IS 'SURE'

(ii)   Civil proceedings

In virtually all other proceedings – claims for damages, regulatory/disciplinary proceedings – the claim or allegation has to be proved on the balance of probabilities, that is it must be made out so that it is more likely than not. If it is not, then the claim or complaint is not proved. In a claim for damages, even if the claimant shows that it is more likely than not that the defendant was in breach of duty, it is still necessary to prove the amount of damages to which he is entitled, and each head of damages (i.e. category of loss) must be established on the balance of probabilities.

It is theoretically possible that at the end of the case both sides' cases are evenly balanced so that the claimant will lose. However the appeal courts have pointed out on several occasions that this should not happen and a judge should be able to make up his mind one way or the other.

Once in such a case something is found to be more likely than not, that is it is established 'on the balance of probabilities', then it is proved for all purposes in the proceedings to which the 'balance of probabilities' test applies. In that sense 51% probability is enough to amount to absolute proof in such proceedings, although in practice a decision is unlikely to be that finely balanced. The courts recognise that this is a result which will seem strange to anyone with a scientific background, where finding something to be 'probable' is a long way short of finding it proved. However in those proceedings to which the balance of probabilities applies, once something is found to be more probable than not, that is the end of the matter.

> *In our legal system, if a judge finds it more likely than not that something did take place, then it is treated as having taken place. If he finds it more likely than not that it did not take place, then it is treated as not having taken place. He is not allowed to sit on the fence. He has to find for one side or the other. Sometimes the burden of proof will come to his rescue: the party with the burden of showing that something took place will not have satisfied him that it did. But generally speaking a judge is able to make up his mind where the truth lies without needing to rely upon the burden of proof*[2].

IN A CIVIL OR FAMILY CASE, PROOF IS ON THE BALANCE OF PROBABILITIES. THEREFORE THE FACT FINDER MUST BE SATISFIED IF SOMETHING IS SHOWN TO BE 'MORE LIKELY THAN NOT'

In a coroners' court at an inquest we will see that the law has until very recently been that the standard of proof may be either the criminal or civil standard depending on the nature of the facts. A recent court decision that the normal civil standard of proof applies in the case of a verdict of suicide, a decision which should now logically be extended to a verdict of unlawful killing, throws doubt on that previous position so that the standard may now be the civil standard in all cases (see Section 15.8(iii) below).

---

2   *In re B (Children) (FC)* [2008] UKHL 35 at para 32

5

The court system

The court (and tribunal) system of England and Wales is a maze, which most lawyers, with the help of the occasional reference to a legal handbook of one kind or another, will be equipped to find their way round. A clinician however will be led through the maze by others, should the need arise, but this Chapter will attempt to take some of the mystery out of finding the important landmarks within the maze.

The following flow chart sets out the structure of the courts and tribunals in England and Wales and is from www.judiciary.gov.uk.

The structure of the courts

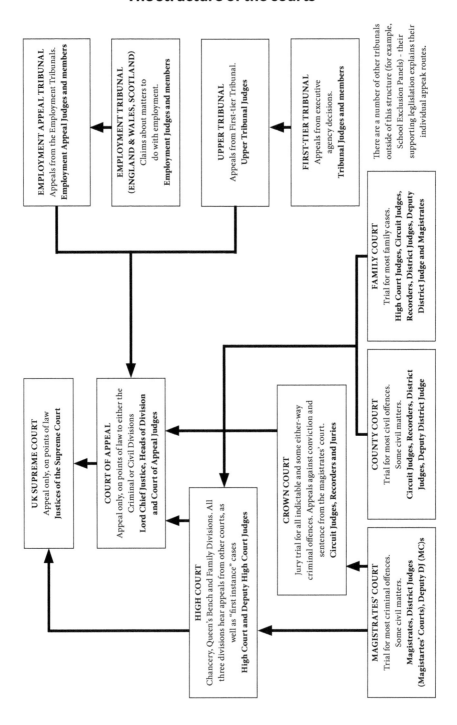

EMPLOYMENT APPEAL TRIBUNAL. Appeals from the Employment Tribunals. **Employment Appeal Judges and members**

EMPLOYMENT TRIBUNAL (ENGLAND & WALES, SCOTLAND) Claims about matters to do with employment. **Employment Judges and members**

UPPER TRIBUNAL. Appeals from First-tier Tribunal. **Upper Tribunal Judges**

FIRST-TIER TRIBUNAL. Appeals from executive agency decisions. **Tribunal Judges and members**

There are a number of other tribunals outside of this structure (for example, School Exclusion Panels) – their supporting legislation explains their individual appeak routes.

FAMILY COURT Trial for most family cases. **High Court Judges, Circuit Judges, Recorders, District Judges, Deputy District Judge and Magistrates**

UK SUPREME COURT Appeal only, on points of law **Justices of the Supreme Court**

COURT OF APPEAL Appeal only, on points of law to either the Criminal or Civil Divisions **Lord Chief Justice, Heads of Division and Court of Appeal Judges**

CROWN COURT Jury trial for all indictable and some either-way criminal offences. Appeals against conviction and sentence from the magistrates' court. **Circuit Judges, Recorders and Juries**

COUNTY COURT Trial for most civil offences. Some civil matters. **Circuit Judges, Recorders, District Judges, Deputy District Judge**

HIGH COURT Chancery, Queen's Bench and Family Divisions. All three divisions hear appeals from other courts, as well as "first instance" cases **High Court and Deputy High Court Judges**

MAGISTRATES' COURT Trial for most criminal offences. Some civil matters. **Magistrates, District Judges (Magistrates' Courts), Deputy DJ (MC)s**

As the judiciary website explains:

Our courts system is complicated and – in places – confusing, because it has developed over 1,000 years rather than being designed from scratch.

Different types of case are dealt with in specific courts: for example, all criminal cases will start in the magistrates' court, but the more serious criminal matters are committed (or sent) to the Crown Court. Appeals from the Crown Court will go to the High Court, and potentially to the Court of Appeal or even the Supreme Court.

Civil cases will sometimes be dealt with by magistrates, but may well go to a county court. Again, appeals will go to the High Court and then to the Court of Appeal – although to different divisions of those courts.

The tribunals system has its own structure for dealing with cases and appeals, but decisions from different chambers of the Upper Tribunal, and the Employment Appeals Tribunal, may also go to the Court of Appeal.

The courts structure covers England and Wales; the tribunals system covers England, Wales, and in some cases Northern Ireland and Scotland.

For most practical purposes and in relation to the contact that a healthcare professional is likely to have with the system, the courts can be slightly simplified:

Civil claims (principally money claims) are commenced in the County Court for lower value claims and the High Court for higher value claims, the crossover point commonly being at or above a figure of several hundred thousand pounds. There is the ability for each of those courts to transfer a case to the other in appropriate circumstances. The procedural judge and the judge hearing the lower value and more straightforward cases is the District Judge (addressed as 'sir' or 'madam') in the County Court and the Master (male or female) (addressed as 'Master') in the High Court. The trial judge in the County Court is a Circuit Judge or Recorder (part time judge) (addressed as 'Your Honour'). In the High Court, the trial judge is a High Court Judge or Deputy High Court Judge (part time) (addressed as 'My Lord' or 'My Lady').

Criminal cases are commenced in the Magistrates' Court. Less serious cases are tried there, before either lay magistrates (generally three) or a District Judge (Magistrates' Court), who is a full time judge (and all are addressed as 'sir' or 'madam'). More serious cases are sent on to the Crown Court where, depending to some extent on the seriousness of the case, they are tried by a High Court Judge, Circuit Judge or Recorder, all of whom sit with a jury (the judge addressed as in the civil courts). A jury determines whether a defendant is guilty or not guilty and the judge alone determines the sentence or other penalty following a finding of guilt.

Family cases, mainly concerned with the wellbeing of children or property disputes on divorce, are generally commenced in the Family Court, which assigns the case to a judge considered appropriate for the issues involved, ranging from High Court Judge to lay magistrates, and including all of the judges mentioned above except for a Master. More difficult cases may be commenced in the High Court (before a High Court Judge or Deputy).

Tribunals are separate from the Court system although appeals from them (on matters of law only) come back to the Court system. There is also an appeal system in some fields within the tribunal system in which an appeal may be allowed to challenge a finding of fact. Tribunals are intended to be less formal than the courts and more accessible to unrepresented parties.

Coroners' Courts, it will be noted, are outside the Court system. Although prior to 2009 medical practitioners could be appointed coroners, coroners must now be barristers or solicitors of at least 5 years' experience (and are addressed as 'sir' or 'madam'). Each court has its own territorial jurisdiction, the location of a dead body determining which Coroners' Court deals with the matter. A judge may be appointed as a coroner to deal with very high profile or complex cases.

As the chart above indicates there are also a number of tribunals outside the indicated structure established under different pieces of legislation and for different purposes, such as school exclusion panels and professional disciplinary tribunals, although appeals from these on points of law will be back into the Court system, to the High Court.

6

Preparing a witness statement

Chapter outline

The importance of witness statements in seeking to establish past facts in any inquiry into past events has already been referred to several times. In this Chapter witness statements will be looked at more closely and in more detail together with the rules about their content and form. This will enable clinicians to prepare an appropriate and effective draft statement or involve themselves in the statement's drafting with greater understanding of the applicable requirements and the lawyer's objectives.

6.1   Introduction

There are a variety of situations in which healthcare professionals may be asked to prepare, or to assist in the preparation of, a witness statement addressing an event which has occurred and in which they have been involved. This may be part of an inquiry such as a serious incident investigation, in relation to a coroner's inquest, court proceedings or criminal investigations, for professional regulatory proceedings or for other disciplinary hearings. Before use in proceedings it is to be expected that lawyers acting for the witness, or for a party in support of whose case the witness statement is prepared, will have input into the final format and that they will ensure that it complies with any procedural require- ments of such proceedings. Nevertheless it is advantageous for the healthcare professional to produce the first draft in a clear and useful format to ensure that the statement provides the clearest and most accurate evidence possible.

Once a statement has been made it should be assumed that anyone can have access to it, and that it will be available to compare with any subsequent evidence given by the witness. That is not always the case and depending on the purpose for which it has been obtained it may be that in some circumstances confidential- ity in it ('privilege') can be claimed by the party on whose behalf it is obtained. Any inconsistencies between statements or between a statement and subsequent oral evidence are likely to detract severely from the reliability of the evidence in the eyes of any tribunal (see Section 2.5 above). It is therefore important that the witness is sure that the statement accurately relates the facts and is the evidence that the witness would give on oath.

6.2 Content

A witness statement should be written in readily understood language and should generally reflect the language of the witness. However technical terms should be restricted to those which are necessary and they must be explained as appropriate. Only evidence which is necessary for the purpose for which the witness statement is required should be included and in many cases this purpose will be defined in an early paragraph of the witness statement. Exaggeration and speculation must always be avoided.

The witness statement should generally reflect what the witness can give direct evidence of, that is what the witness has seen, said or heard directly, or done herself. Hearsay (see Section 3.1(ii) above) may be acceptable, depending on the purpose of the witness statement and its use, but it is important to make clear what part of the evidence is hearsay, that is what is being given in evidence on the basis of what someone has told the witness, and the circumstances in which that evidence came to the knowledge of the witness. It is also important to be clear about the circumstances in which the direct (non-hearsay) evidence was received. The active voice – 'I did this' – is therefore much more useful than the passive voice – 'this was done' – as it makes clear who did what, and also gives the witness 'ownership' of the events described.

If in the witness statement it is necessary to address a decision which was made by or involving the witness, then it is important to identify precisely the facts relied upon at the time in making the decision, and the reasoning of the witness (at that time) resulting in the decision. If the decision was in part based on infor- mation provided by someone else (hearsay), then it is important to explain that that was the case and why it was considered reasonable to rely on that informa- tion. If facts which subsequently came to light are relied on retrospectively as justifying actions or a decision, then it must be made clear that those facts were not known at the time, even if they were assumed or inferred, in which case that should also be explained.

A witness statement is a statement of fact – what happened – and should not include expressions of opinion. That does not exclude giving evidence of opinions formed in the past and upon which a treatment decision was made, as that is treated as a fact – the fact that the opinion was (in the past) formed. (Giving opinions as an expert witness are considered in Chapter 7 below 'Acting as an Expert'.)

The statement should follow chronological order as far as possible in setting out the relevant facts.

> A WITNESS STATEMENT SHOULD CONTAIN ALL
> THE EVIDENCE THE WITNESS COULD GIVE IN
> ORAL EVIDENCE AND WHICH IS RELEVANT TO THE
> ISSUES IT ADDRESSES

In providing a draft witness statement to the legal team the witness should concentrate on accuracy, completeness and comprehensibility, and be concerned less at that stage with the legal niceties as to the rules of evidence, which it is for the lawyers to help the witness address.

The witness statement should be the complete evidence of the witness on the matters in dispute or relevant to the proceedings or process. It should be presumed that there will be no opportunity to expand upon it subsequently, even if sometimes there will be. In most proceedings the witness statement will stand as the witness's evidence in chief, that is the evidence given to the side or party calling the witness, and therefore will stand as the witness's evidence subject to any cross-examination by the opposing side.

If lawyers (or anyone else, including for example police officers) become involved in drafting the witness statement, it is very important, whatever pressures may be placed on the statement maker, expressly or impliedly, that the maker is happy to sign off the witness statement as being true and honestly made. That is what the witness will generally be required to confirm, commonly on oath, before relying on the witness statement in any non-criminal proceedings or process, and that is what is stated in the declaration which the witness will sign in a witness statement in criminal proceedings. Any inaccuracies or inconsistencies between the witness's evidence and the witness statement are likely to be the subject of cross examination and an attack on the witness's credibility, and even the witness's honesty.

6.3   Form

The form of the witness statement will be different in the different courts, tribunals, panels and hearings for which it is used, and guidance will usually be given by the person seeking the witness statement and, if not provided, should be sought. Generally statements in criminal proceedings are in a different format to others.

(i)   Non-criminal proceedings

If the witness statement is being prepared for the purposes of existing proceedings or some existing procedural process, the statement starts by setting out as a heading the formal name of those proceedings or the process, which may appear on other documents relating to that process. After that should come the full name and professional address of the witness.

The content of the statement should then follow in numbered paragraphs, starting with an explanation as to the purpose for which the statement is being made and the witness's relevant qualifications, expertise and role in the matter being addressed. Thereafter, so far as is possible, in relating past events the paragraphs should be in chronological order, that is the witness statement should 'tell the story'.

Pages, like paragraphs, should also be numbered. This is for ease of use by lawyers and the court and to enable speedy identification of a particular point within the statement of a particular matter referred to in the statement.

It is sometimes useful to use headings within the statement to guide the reader, whether they be references to times or dates, or different aspects of the evidence.

Documents referred to, such as medical records, should not be set out in full within the witness statement, but should be identified and as appropriate the relevant part identified or quoted, and if convenient a copy page containing the relevant part can be attached, along with all other relevant copy documents, at the end of the witness statement. These 'exhibits' are commonly identified by using the statement maker's initials and a number (eg 'GSE 1') and marking the copy with this. One exhibit can contain a number of pages, so that all copy medical records, or all medical records of one category, considered relevant could be given one identifier, and the pages then numbered to provide a clear reference for each page referred to in the text (eg 'see page 7 of 'GSE 1"). Contemporaneous records setting out what the witness did and why are particularly useful in providing an account of events in a witness statement - hence the importance of accurate and full records (see Chapter 8 'Records and Making Notes' below).

Although different proceedings require different formalities, in the absence of other guidance the statement should conclude with a paragraph stating 'I believe that the facts stated in this witness statement are true', followed by a signature and date. The statement should only be signed if it is true and known to be true by the witness/statement maker.

(ii)   Criminal proceedings

A form for a witness statement in criminal proceedings is available online[1], and looks as follows:

STATEMENT OF WITNESS

(Criminal Procedure Rules, r. 27.2;

Criminal Justice Act 1967, s. 9, Magistrates' Courts Act 1980, s.5B)

STATEMENT OF..

Age of witness (if over 18, enter "over 18"): ....

This statement (consisting of ...... pages) **is true to the best of my knowledge and belief and I make it knowing that, if it is tendered in evidence, I shall be liable to prosecution if I have wilfully stated in it anything which I know to be false, or do not believe to be true.**

[BODY OF STATEMENT]

Signed: .... (witness)

Date: ....

---

1   http://www.justice.gov.uk/courts/procedure-rules/criminal/docs/october-2015/ws001-eng. doc

It is important to appreciate that the effect of the declaration is that stating anything dishonestly in the witness statement will amount to perjury and could lead to prosecution.

The first paragraph should be an introduction, setting out the clinician's name and basic and any higher qualifications, the name of the organisation employing the clinician and the position of the clinician within the organisation, and the duration of employment.

The statement will normally be based on the patient's records or other documentation produced by the Trust, and the sources of the evidence on which the statement is based should be identified (an examination, A&E notes, hospital notes, results of investigations). The statement must be clear as to who examined the patient and if it was not the statement maker, identify who did, and any reason why that person is not making the statement.

The patient about whom the statement is made must be identified together with the date, time and place of any examination, and the reason for the examination. Where the history of events leading up to the examination are given, it is important to identify who gave that history, and details of any allegations made.

The patient's past medical history will not normally be relevant. In criminal proceedings the evidence required from the clinician is most likely to be about the condition of the patient at the time of the relevant examination, and grounds will not exist for releasing confidential information about the patient's past history (see Chapters 10 and 11 below).

The examination is likely to be important evidence and details should be provided, for example, of any injury, its site, its dimensions and its effects on any other structures. Where there are a number of injuries, they should be numbered for easy reference and each one should be dealt with separately.

Details of any treatment and of any advice given should be provided.

As this is the witness statement of a witness of fact and not of an expert, opinion should not be included unless the statement maker is expressly asked to provide one and has the expertise to be able to provide the opinion sought. For example it is not appropriate to express an opinion on the nature of a weapon used or the mode of an assault unless the clinician has the necessary expertise to do so and can evidence that expertise.

Before releasing confidential information about the patient, the clinician must be satisfied that one of the grounds for doing so applies (see Chapters 10 and 11 below). Most commonly this will be the consent of the patient or public interest where a serious crime has been committed.

Further reading

Guidance on the format for a witness statement in a civil case (justice.gov.uk)[2]

Providing a Witness Statement for the Police (RCEM February 2012) [3]

---

2   https://www.justice.gov.uk/courts/procedure-rules/civil/standard-directions/general/witness-statements

3   https://www.rcem.ac.uk/docs/College Guidelines/5z15. Providing a witness statement for the Police (Feb 2012).pdf

7

Acting as an expert witness

Chapter outline

Acting as an expert witness, and that encompasses providing an expert report or advice as an expert for the purposes of proceedings as well as giving evidence at a hearing, brings into play numerous rules with which the expert must comply. Breaches of these rules can have a serious impact on the clinician's career, not just as an expert but in their everyday professional work. A breach of a requirement imposed on a clinician in giving expert evidence can result in an investigation of professional fitness to practise. This Chapter looks at the nature of the evidence clinicians acting as experts can give in any proceedings, inquiry or other process, when expert evidence is allowed and for what purpose, who is an expert for these purposes, and where the rules applicable to different courts and other processes can be found.

7.1 Introduction

The purpose for which expert witnesses are used is to give evidence based on their expertise, to explain relevant matters for which their expertise is needed and to express opinions based on (and within) their expertise. The expert witness therefore helps the court (or jury or tribunal) to decide issues that are beyond its (or their) technical knowledge or expertise. An expert has an overriding duty to a court (or tribunal) to be independent and objective and to assist the court (or tribunal) with matters within the expert's expertise.

Clinicians can provide their skills as expert witnesses when assisting in investigations carried out within their employer healthcare provider (such as a serious incident investigation or internal disciplinary proceedings) or for the purposes of civil or criminal cases, fitness to practise investigations or a coroner's inquest. (We consider the nature of those processes in Chapter 15 below).

Expert witness work can be the source of a significant private income for the clinician, and it is also the opportunity to provide and to justify opinions within a forensic context which appeals to many, although by no means all, clinicians.

A full exploration of this topic is well beyond the confines of this general work. However in this Chapter the main frameworks within the English jurisdiction which govern such expert witness work will be noted. Healthcare professionals providing expert evidence in these jurisdictions are required to know and to comply with the relevant Rules and practice directions. There is no scope for an amateurish approach to such work, which would almost certainly amount to professional misconduct as well as being penalised in the court or tribunal in which the expert is appearing. Such penalties may include financial penalties on the expert witness personally, as well as the risk of being reported to the expert witness's professional body.

(i) Contrasting factual and opinion evidence

Witnesses may not give evidence of their opinion on a matter unless they have an expertise which validates that opinion and the court or tribunal has consented to expert evidence being given either by someone with expertise in that particular field or by a named expert. Otherwise a witness's evidence must be limited to matters of a factual nature. As experts, witnesses may only give evidence of matters within their area of expertise. Where a clinician is being criticised for some action or inaction, the clinician's evidence will normally be limited to factual evidence about what occurred and why the action or inaction resulted. The expert is called to express an opinion as to whether, based on the facts as they are known or believed to be, the action or inaction of the clinician fell below the standard reasonably to be expected of a reasonably competent clinician.

> A WITNESS CAN ONLY GIVE OPINION EVIDENCE
> ON MATTERS WITHIN THE WITNESS'S EXPERTISE
> AND WITH THE COURT'S/TRIBUNAL'S PERMISSION

It is generally assumed that clinicians instructed to provide expert reports for use in proceedings are hired only in order to provide opinion evidence. That assumption is wrong. Expert evidence is multi-faceted, and experts can give evidence in a number of ways, and recognition of that fact will impact on the approach to report writing by the expert, the manner in which the report is constructed by the expert, and the manner in which the report may be de-constructed in cross-examination.

Typically an expert is instructed in litigation to provide opinion evidence – has the standard of care fallen below that reasonably to be expected of a reasonably competent expert in that field, or has any injury, loss or damage been caused by a breach of duty, or what is the extent of injury, loss or damage resulting from an accident or other adverse event? But that is not the full picture and there are other types of expert evidence which may be just as important to lawyers and to judges and tribunals hearing the cases, and which are frequently contained within an expert's court report.

The expert should therefore be aware of the different roles that an expert may have as a court expert and the separate, but often overlapping, reasons why the expert may have been instructed. This was considered recently in the Supreme Court decision in *Kennedy v Cordia (Services) LLP*[1] which was concerned with the evidence of an engineer in relation to a slipping case. Although dealing with an appeal from Scotland, the Court's observations are equally applicable to England and Wales and to medical experts.

(ii)   The expert as witness of fact

Like any other witness the medical expert may be an expert of fact giving evidence of what she observed, so long as it is relevant to a fact in issue in the case. So a doctor may give evidence of an examination of the claimant or patient, or the appearance or movements of the claimant or patient on arriving or leaving the consulting room. Like any other witness of fact, it is important, particularly if the evidence may be challenged, that in addition to giving the factual evidence, the medical expert also gives evidence as to the circumstances in which the facts were ascertained. For example, in relation to the clinical encounter with the claimant or patient, the report should include the time spent together with any circumstances potentially supportive of the reliability of the expert's account, or in the case of other observations, information as to how long the person was observed, from what distance, whether the view was unobstructed and what the lighting conditions were.

---

1   *Kennedy v Cordia (Services) LLP* [2016] UKSC 6, http://www.bailii.org/uk/cases/UKSC/2016/6.html

(iii)   The expert as witness of expert facts

As a skilled witness, an expert may also give evidence based on her knowledge and experience of a subject matter, drawing on the work of others, such as the findings of published research or the pooled knowledge of a team of people with whom she works. A medical expert may therefore, for example, give evidence as to how a joint functions and the potential impact on the joint or on bone of a particular fracture or disease, or of what is found to be present but not immediately apparent (for example by palpation). This may well not be opinion evidence, but evidence of facts known to and shared by similar experts. For such evidence to be admissible from the witness, the same rules that govern admissibility of expert opinion evidence also apply. Therefore to be permitted to give this evidence, the skilled witness must set out her qualifications, by training and experience, to give expert evidence (most probably covered in the CV section of the report) and also say from where she has obtained information if it is not based on her own observations and experience.

This expert factual evidence may be given by itself or in combination with, or as the basis for giving, opinion evidence.

(iv)   The expert expressing opinion as to 'missing' facts

Sometimes the expert is required to, or identifies the need to, express opinion as to what the facts were (on the balance of probabilities). For example, there may be missing observations or readings in the clinical records or missing or absent x-rays or other images, the content of which might be important in providing an opinion. Based on other information or data, and expert knowledge, the surgeon may be able to express an opinion as to what that absent fact was (to the appropriate standard of proof – see Section 4.2 above).

To provide such an opinion as to the 'missing' fact experts must be able to justify their expertise to do so. That is probably covered by the expert's standard CV section of the report, but if not, then the expertise must be expressly addressed.

(v)   The expert giving 'pure' opinion evidence

'Pure' opinion evidence, in contrast to expert factual evidence, will address, for example in medical expert evidence, condition and prognosis, causation or standard of care. This is what is normally thought of when referring to expert evidence.

(vi)   Expert evidence and 'the ultimate issue'

It used to be the law that an expert could not give an opinion on the 'ultimate issue' which a jury was required to decide in a case. The rule is now much less rigorously applied but the expert witness should be aware of the rule and of its significance.

The 'ultimate issue' is the final question which the jury has to determine in the case in order to return a verdict (of guilty or not guilty in a criminal case or proved or not in a civil case) and for an expert to address this issue would be to usurp the role of the jury. So in a trial of a defendant on a charge of gross negligence manslaughter (see Section 15.6(i) below), it would not be appropriate for the expert to express an opinion as to the guilt or innocence of the defendant and it used not to be appropriate for the expert to address an opinion as to whether the negligence alleged was properly regarded as 'gross'. In civil cases we rarely now see juries, and judges hearing a case on their own are usually not too concerned if an expert does address the ultimate issue. In expressing an opinion as to whether or not the standard of care fell below that of a reasonably competent practitioner in that field (the Bolam test – see Section 15.5 below) an expert should not express an opinion on the 'ultimate issue' as to whether or not the practitioner was 'negligent' as that is a matter of law for the judge, but that decision will flow inevitably from the decision as to whether the standard of care fell below the standard identified by the expert, which the expert's opinion directly and expressly does address.

In a criminal case, greater care is needed when the expert addresses the ultimate issue. On a criminal appeal[2] in 1993 it was said that:

> if there is such a prohibition [in addressing the ultimate issue] it has long been more honoured in the breach than the observance. … Since counsel can bring the witness so close to opining on the ultimate issue that the inference as to his view is obvious, the rule can only be… a matter of form rather than substance. In our view an expert is called to give his opinion and he should be allowed to do so. It is however important that the judge should make clear to the jury that they are not bound by the expert's opinion and that the issue is for them to decide.

In *R v Pora*[3] the court[4] was concerned with a psychologist who gave evidence as to the unreliability of a confession in relation to a criminal allegation. It was emphasised that it was the duty of an expert witness to provide material on which a court can form its own conclusions on relevant issues.

> The expert witness should be careful to recognise, however, the need to avoid supplanting the court's role as the ultimate decision-maker on matters that are central to the outcome of the case ….

The court concluded that:-

> in general, an expert should only be called on to express an opinion on the 'ultimate issue' where that is necessary in order that his evidence provide substantial help to the trier of the fact.

---

2   *R v Stockwell* [1993] 97 Cr App R 260

3   [2015] UKPC 9

4   The Privy Council which consists of judges of the Supreme Court hearing appeals from countries outside the UK

The expert therefore can address all those matters which might render the confession unreliable in the particular case but should not express an opinion on the matter the court had to decide, the 'ultimate issue', that is whether the confession was in fact unreliable.

Expert witnesses in the trial of David Sellu[5] (a colorectal consultant convicted of manslaughter on the basis of his gross negligence causing the death of a patient) were repeatedly asked whether the negligence, or the falling below the standard of a reasonably competent colorectal consultant, was 'gross', and on a significant number of occasions stated that that was their opinion. The fact that they were allowed to give this evidence (and therefore to express an opinion on something which sounded perilously close to the ultimate issue – whether the negligence was gross) was not a ground of appeal. However the appeal was allowed (and the conviction quashed)[6] because the judge did not adequately direct the jury on the meaning of gross negligence for the purpose of establishing manslaughter (see Section 15.6(i) below).

(vii)   Rules as to admissibility of expert evidence

Civil courts, criminal courts, inquests and tribunals have different rules about when and how expert evidence is admissible in evidence.

Underlying the approach in each kind of proceedings, and whether the expert is giving skilled evidence of fact or expert opinion, the admissibility of the skilled evidence is governed by the same four considerations:

1.   Will the evidence assist the court in its task?

2.   Does the witness have the necessary knowledge and experience?

3.   Is the witness impartial in the presentation and assessment of the evidence?

4.   Is there a reliable body of knowledge or experience to underpin the expert's evidence?

But opinion evidence, in contrast to factual evidence, is only admissible if it is necessary, rather than merely of assistance, for the court to have such evidence in order to resolve the matter in dispute. For example in a civil claim, medical expert opinion evidence to address condition and prognosis, causation or standard of care is normally necessary, and that it is necessary is obvious. However medical expert opinion to address missing facts is not necessarily obvious and has to be justified – the report would need to spell out why it is necessary to establish the missing fact, as well as justifying the expert's expertise to provide it.

---

5   [2016] EWCA Crim 1716

6   Other grounds of appeal based on new expert evidence were rejected

(viii)   Who is 'an expert'?

It will be apparent from the preceding paragraphs that the core qualifications to be an expert witness are:

- To have the necessary knowledge and experience to provide an expert opinion on the matter on which the expert is instructed
- To be impartial (that is to have no conflict of interest and no likely bias)
- To have knowledge of, and to understand, the rules governing the giving of expert evidence in that particular court, tribunal or other process.

An expert is also required to be competent in writing expert reports and giving expert evidence.

It follows that a practitioner must have sufficient relevant training and experience in the field of expertise required in the particular circumstances of the dispute or inquiry not only to be able to provide (and justify) an opinion, but to be able to confront and challenge if necessary the opinion given by an experienced expert acting for an opposing party.

Further guidance about the requirements to present oneself as a court expert, specifically in the civil courts but of more general application, will be found in the book referred to in the following Section.

7.2   Civil procedure rules

The relevant rules are set out in Part 35 of the Civil Procedure Rules 1998. Rules and guidance appear within Rule 35[7], the practice direction to Part 35[8] and the Guidance for the Instruction of Experts in Civil Claims 2014[9].

Readers are referred to this author's and Lynden Alexander's book *'Writing Medico-Legal Reports in Civil Claims – an essential guide*[10] for more information about medical expert work in relation to civil claims and the Civil Procedure Rules, including report writing skills and the development of an expert witness practice.

7.3   Family procedure rules

The relevant rules are set out in Part 25 of the Family Procedure Rules 2010[11] and Practice directions 25A to 25F.

---

7   http://www.justice.gov.uk/courts/procedure-rules/civil/rules/part35

8   http://www.justice.gov.uk/courts/procedure-rules/civil/rules/part35/pd_part35

9   https://www.judiciary.gov.uk/wp-content/uploads/2014/08/experts-guidance-cjc-aug-2014-amended-dec-8.pdf

10   Purchased through www.prosols.uk.com 2nd edition 2015

11   http://www.justice.gov.uk/courts/procedure-rules/family/parts/part_25

7.4   Criminal procedure rules

The relevant rules are set out in Part 19 of the Criminal Procedure Rules 2015[12] and Criminal Practice Directions Division V[13].

7.5   Court of protection

The relevant rules are set out in Part 15 of the Court of Protection Rules 2017[14] and Practice Direction 15A[15].

7.6   Medical practicitioners' tribunal service

There is guidance for expert witnesses appearing before the Tribunal in 'Protocol for the instruction of experts to give evidence in Medical Practitioners Tribunal hearings'[16].

7.7   Other forums

There are many tribunals dealing with a wide range of topics including social welfare, education, immigration, employment and regulatory matters as well as a system of arbitrations. If asked to provide expert evidence for any of these it is important to inquire if there are any specific rules about the nature, extent and format of expert evidence, and fees payable. If there are none, then generally the safest course is to follow the principles underlying the Civil Procedure Rules so far as is practical.

---

12   http://www.justice.gov.uk/courts/procedure-rules/criminal/docs/2015/crim-proc-rules-2015-part-19.pdf

13   https://www.justice.gov.uk/courts/procedure-rules/criminal/practice-direction/2015/crim-practice-directions-V-evidence-2015.pdf

14   http://www.legislation.gov.uk/uksi/2017/1035/part/15/made

15   https://www.judiciary.gov.uk/wp-content/uploads/2014/05/pd-15a-expert-evidence.pdf

16   https://www.mpts-uk.org/DC8269_MPTS_expert_witness_protocol_58818768.pdf

8

Records and making notes

Chapter outline

Having seen how a lawyer's mind works and the lawyer's approach to, and method for weighing, evidence this Chapter will look at how clinical records and notes can better record not only what has happened but, by referencing the thought processes applied, can better explain why diagnoses or decisions are made. Subsequent inquiry into the events will be better informed, and the clinician will be better able to provide a reasoned and full account of treatment and diagnosis. Discussions with patients can then convincingly be recalled and described.

This Chapter will look at what records should contain, how the normal and routine should be recorded, what to record when nothing significant is found, how to explain decisions and how to provide a record after a significant event.

8.1   Introduction

Clinical records and notes are often crucial to professional colleagues to whom a patient is passed or referred. There is no excuse for ambiguity or uncertainty in the information passed on, let alone inaccuracy, the consequences of which might be serious for the patient.

Clinical records and notes will be released to lawyers if they are relevant to proceedings which are underway, but also where they may prove relevant to proceedings which have not yet been commenced. For example, if, following an adverse outcome giving rise to questions as to the standard of care received by a patient, a clinical negligence claim is being considered against a healthcare professional or a healthcare provider, until the records and notes have been seen it is normally not possible for lawyer or medical expert to advise with any degree of confidence whether commencing proceedings can be justified.

From a lawyer's point of view when looking back at events through such records, they should contain not just key events of particular significance, and a check list of actions, checks or advice but:

- The very normal - normal observations as to consciousness, temperature, response, blood count etc – to show that the observations were made
- Absences – something which is not seen, noted or recorded but might be of relevance if seen – no loss of consciousness, no raised temperature, no abnormality in blood count etc
- An explanation of opinions formed or decisions made, including decisions to do nothing
- They should, so far as is possible within the constraints of record keeping during busy clinical practice, 'tell the story' so as to provide a picture, which would be understood by another similar healthcare professional, of what took place and why.

8.2   Contents of records

Medical records include both handwritten and electronic records, correspondence with health professionals, laboratory reports and imaging records and printouts from monitoring equipment. They also include communications with the patient and with other clinicians involved in the care of the patient.

The main reason for maintaining medical records is to ensure continuity of care for the patient. However from a lawyer's viewpoint they are crucial in investigating complaints or allegations of breach of duty on the party of the clinician, providing a contemporaneous account and providing evidence to explain what happened, or did not happen, and evidence of the decisions made or opinions reached (or sometimes not made or reached) and the reasons for the decisions and opinions (or not making or reaching them). They may also show inconsistencies which can undermine the evidence or record-making of an individual. Contemporaneous (or near-contemporaneous) records are likely to provide the most reliable evidence of what took place and the factors relevant to any decisions made, as well as being the best memory-refreshing tool when the clinician seeks to re-create events months or years later.

Good Medical Practice (GMC) gives the following guidance (at paras 19 and 21):-

> *Documents you make (including clinical records) to formally record your work must be clear, accurate and legible. You should make records at the same time as the events you are recording or as soon as possible afterwards.*
>
> *Clinical records should include:*
>
> a) *relevant clinical findings*
>
> b) *the decisions made and the actions agreed, and who is making the decisions and agreeing the actions*
>
> c) *the information given to patients*
>
> d) *any drugs prescribed or other investigation or treatment*
>
> e) *who is making the record and when[1].*

Good Surgical Practice (RCS) goes further and provides more detail in its guidance (at para 1.3):

> *Surgeons must ensure that accurate, comprehensive, legible and contemporaneous records are maintained of all their interactions with patients. In meeting the standards of Good Medical Practice you should:*
>
> • *Be fully versed in the use of the electronic health record system used in your organisation and record clinical information in a way that can be shared with colleagues and patients and reused safely in an electronic environment.*
>
> • *Take part in the mandatory training on information governance offered by your organisation, including training on data protection and access to health records.*
>
> • *Ensure that all medical records are accurate, clear, legible, comprehensive and contemporaneous and have the patient's identification details on them.*
>
> • *Ensure that when members of the surgical team make casenote entries these are legibly signed and show the date, and, in cases where the*

---

1   https://www.gmc-uk.org/-/media/documents/Good_medical_practice___English_1215.pdf_51527435.pdf

clinical condition is changing, the correct time.

- *Ensure that a record is made of the name of the most senior surgeon seeing the patient at each postoperative visit.*

- *Ensure that a record is made by a member of the surgical team of important events and communications with the patient or supporter (for example, prognosis or potential complication). Any change in the treatment plan should be recorded.*

- *Ensure that there are clear (preferably typed) operative notes for every procedure. The notes should accompany the patient into recovery and to the ward and should give sufficient detail to enable continuity of care by another doctor. The notes should include:*

  - *Date and time*

  - *Elective/emergency procedure*

  - *Names of the operating surgeon and assistant*

  - *Name of the theatre anaesthetist*

  - *Operative procedure carried out*

  - *Incision*

  - *Operative diagnosis*

  - *Operative findings*

  - *Any problems/complications*

  - *Any extra procedure performed and the reason why it was performed*

  - *Details of tissue removed, added or altered*

  - *Identification of any prosthesis used, including the serial numbers of prostheses and other implanted materials*

  - *Details of closure technique*

  - *Anticipated blood loss*

  - *Antibiotic prophylaxis (where applicable)*

  - *DVT prophylaxis (where applicable)*

- *Detailed postoperative care instructions*

- *Signature*

- *Ensure that sufficiently detailed follow-up notes and discharge summaries are completed to allow another doctor to assess the care of the patient at any time*

- *Ensure that you are familiar and fully compliant with the guidelines of the Data Protection Act 1998 around the use and storage of all patient identifiable information[2].*

Although specifically aimed at surgeons, this emphasis (with examples) on providing a complete record of all material matters, and on accuracy, clarity, legibility, comprehensiveness and contemporaneousness, is applicable, and should be regarded as obligatory, across all clinical areas.

> RECORDS MUST BE ACCURATE, CLEAR, LEGIBLE, COMPREHENSIVE AND CONTEMPORANEOUS

8.3   The normal and routine, and 'standard practice'

Records should contain the normal and the routine. If it is disputed on a subsequent investigation that a doctor carried out a thorough examination of a patient, and the records indicate only that blood pressure was noted to be slightly raised, then the contemporaneous records do not support the doctor's case given by her orally that all of the other aspects of a 'thorough examination' were carried out, even if the doctor's assertion is that everything else was normal and did not merit recording. The 'normal' findings are as important to record as the 'abnormal' if the patient's condition at that time subsequently becomes an important issue.

If 'usual advice given' is recorded, or 'head injury advice given' is noted, and a question arises as to what actual advice was given on this particular occasion, the record provides poor support for having given any particular item of advice. If the patient (or family member) subsequently denies that a specific (and in the context, crucial) piece of advice was given, the record will be of far greater assistance to the clinician in supporting the case that complete advice was given if it lists, however briefly, and using whatever shorthand is most useful to the clinician, the items of advice and indicates, by a ✓ or other mark, that on the face of it the specific item of advice was given.

---

2   https://www.rcseng.ac.uk/-/media/files/rcs/standards-and-research/gsp/gsp-2014-web.pdf

To rely on following 'standard practice' as a reason for not making a complete record or for not listing (however briefly) the steps taken runs the risk, if a dispute arises as to what happened, of being unable to prove exactly what occurred. It is routine and standard practice which can (and often does) go wrong, or which accidentally is not followed fully, without the healthcare professional even realising it. The car driver who says 'I always signal when I make that turn so I am sure I would have done on this occasion' is less likely to be believed, if signalling is in dispute, than the driver who describes in detail how and when it was done on that occasion.

Similarly, to record 'neurology intact' or 'distally neurovascularly intact' is to record a conclusion, but to omit the observations which lead to that conclusion. If subsequently there is a dispute, or disagreement, about whether an observation was made, or was accurate, or a subtle variation on normal was observed, the clinician will be in a far stronger position to meet such criticism if the individual observations are recorded as having been made, even if each one is recorded as 'normal'. Again a list, using whatever shorthand is useful to the clinician, with each followed by a ✓ or other sign indicating normality, will be much more supportive of the clinician's conclusion in any subsequent investigation.

It is often said that keeping records is time consuming, and recording standard practice takes time which is not available. A solution is to adopt or devise a system of shorthand, abbreviations and ticks for example, that takes little time to record but acts as both a reminder to do it in the first place and confirmation of each observation or action and, in retrospect, evidence that it was done. For example, acronyms, with ticks against the individual letters, may well suffice.

On a departmental basis the creation of a rubber stamp or other pro forma listing key words, or of an electronic template with boxes to mark with an 'x', can greatly simplify the giving of standard advice, such as standard head injury advice, particularly if supported by the giving of a standard patient information sheet.

None of these approaches is a certain way of proving what was said or done. Boxes can be ticked in the absence of action or advice, and if examined in a courtroom setting, the judge will look at all the evidence, not just the notes and records, if deciding which of 2 versions to find more credible, as we saw in the case of *Hassall* in Chapter 2 above. But thorough record-making is as important a factor in the courtroom as it is to a colleague to whom the care of a patient is suddenly handed.

> RECORD WHAT IS DONE, SEEN AND MEASURED
> EVEN IF IT IS 'NORMAL'

This approach also has the advantage of ensuring that every patient is given all of the routine information that should be given for the patient's well-being.

8.4 Negatives or absence of findings

As with the normal and routine, and standard practice, it is also important to record an absence of findings. A GP examining the baby of a distressed mother and finding nothing of concern in the baby could record 'all normal'; but that would leave the GP open to challenge over precisely what the examination consisted of. A list of 'normal' findings (abbreviation plus ✓ or 'N' or 'OK' or whatever system the doctor prefers) will on the face of it prove that there was a full examination, whatever the mother's subsequent recollection might be. A brief description of the circumstances (such as 'baby distressed/sleepy' and 'mother anxious/tearful') will put the examination in context and may well act as a memory aid when recollecting events some years later.

As we have seen in the previous section, a detailed neurological examination which proves 'normal' is best supported by the list of negative findings, which explain the conclusion.

8.5 Explaining decisions

Making a decision in a clinical setting to do or not to do something is a logical process. Any decision of importance will be based on considering a number of factors (what a lawyer would probably call 'facts'), identifying those that are the material ones, and, as a result of the expertise that the doctor has, applying a reasoning process to those facts and then finally coming to a conclusion or opinion based on that. It is this process – the 'why' - which is most commonly absent from records, and which we will now consider.

By reflecting the decision-making process in the records the clinician provides the best evidence of why the decision was made at that time on the information then available and it will confirm the information on which it was based. It is often the absence of information in the records about what information the doctor had available and why the decision was made that gives rise to claims being made in clinical negligence, or allegations of professional misconduct being brought.

Again this is not a requirement for a lengthy record or note or for a detailed explanation, for which there probably is not time, and which often will not be necessary. But by recording, however briefly, the material facts (factors) taken into account (and possibly why other ones have been discounted), followed by the reasoning (in an abbreviated sentence or two) and the conclusion, there should be no doubt to anyone subsequently reviewing the records why what happened did happen. It also provides the doctor, who may be asked about a routine event some years later, with the best possible note from which to be able to explain and justify the action taken (or not taken).

So, for example, recording 'probably bacterial infection' plus a treatment plan is far less useful than listing briefly the material factors identified from all of the observations taken and previous records made, adding a few words of explanation as to why other explanations have been discounted, and providing the same conclusion. When subsequently questioned about the decision some 3 years later, the doctor will immediately be able to identify confidently the information available when the decision was made and the reasoning process, and so the reason for the decision, and that oral evidence will carry real weight, supported as it will be by the contemporaneous record.

> EXPLAIN DECISION MAKING -
> SHOW YOUR REASONING

In order to make sure that there is enough time available to make such records, it is necessary to devise and use appropriate shorthand or abbreviations and make use of ticks or other signs. But it will also be important consciously to think logically and to practise explaining to others, and briefly, the reasoning that is being applied in making decisions or coming to a conclusion. This will in time minimise the time taken to make such a record. And finally, while on occasions this may be inconvenient, or may take time which could be spent otherwise, it is important to remember the potential assistance to continued professional practice that can be gained from making a record which explains, and supports, actions which have been taken.

8.6   'After the event' records

There may be a number of reasons why the records made at the time of an event are inadequate or incomplete. The significance of factors may not have been appreciated at the time or there may be an emergency which puts record-making to the back of a list of priorities, or perhaps subsequently, because of an unexpected adverse outcome, it is seen that the original records do not do justice to the situation in one way or another.

Para 19 of the GMC's *Good Medical Practice* (quoted above) states that records should be made at the same time as the events being recorded 'or as soon as possible afterwards'. So long as it is apparent that the record being made is not contemporaneous – by dating and timing it, and if appropriate explaining why it is being made – then this can be a useful form of record-making. The events to which the record relates must still be fresh in the maker's mind. The record must genuinely provide more information relevant to the events addressed, and in particular identify material facts (or factors), making clear which were available at the time, and, if any, which subsequently became available. It should also provide a reasoning process and a conclusion or decision. This will again assist the maker in providing a full account of events many months or years later if called upon to do so.

It must not, however, be an 'after the event' justification for the unjustifiable. If it purports to explain and justify something as it happened but contains information only available subsequently then that should be made clear, as it is no longer a near-contemporaneous record but instead a report on an adverse event.

9

Communication

> *You must be honest and trustworthy in all your communication with patients and colleagues. This means you must make clear the limits of your knowledge and make reasonable checks to make sure any information you give is accurate. (Good Medical Practice (GMC) para 68)*

Chapter outline

Long gone are the days when patients meekly accepted the few, often largely incomprehensible, words of the doctor and waited to see what would happen next. This Chapter looks at some of the issues that arise in communicating with patients, their families, other professionals (clinical and legal) and, normally after something untoward has happened, the media.

9.1   Patients

Miscommunication with patients can give rise to misunderstandings which can result in claims or complaints being made against healthcare professionals (as indeed with any professionals). Even if the consequence of such miscommunication does not impact on the clinician, the failure to communicate effectively with the patient will be in breach of the standard expected in Good Medical Practice (GMC) that:

> 31. You must listen to patients, take account of their views, and respond honestly to their questions.
>
> 32. You must give patients the information they want or need to know in a way they can understand. You should make sure that arrangements are made, wherever possible, to meet patients' language and communication needs[1].

It is impossible to involve a patient and her family fully in decisions about care and treatment unless communication is in a manner, at a level, and using language that the patient can understand.

All professionals are prone to using the technical language of their profession, as this is the language they learnt in, communicate with other similar professionals in, and naturally think and write in. It is sometimes felt to be a shorthand (although it probably is not). There is also sometimes a tendency to use such language to 'soften' bad news. It is certainly a way of communicating that excludes those lacking the same training from following fully what is being said or written.

If a patient is told that she is likely to suffer 'some long-term symptoms of significant discomfort' she may not expect to be woken every night as a result of pain with little offered by way of expectation of improvement, and she may well harbour a grievance.

In specifically advising on the language used in an outpatient letter, the Academy of Medical Royal Colleges provides extremely useful guidance and examples in its publication *Please, write to me. Writing outpatient clinic letters to patients. Guidance*[2].

- Avoid the technical, so use 'kidney', not 'renal'
- Avoid acronyms, so use 'Cardiac Resynchronisation Therapy', not 'CRT-D'
- Avoid Latin, so use 'twice daily', not 'bd'.

In terms of style, certainly when writing, but also when speaking:

- Avoid the passive voice and use the active voice – so use 'you decided to have' rather than 'it was decided' or 'the decision was made'
- Use the first and second persons (I and you), so say 'I referred you to' rather than 'a referral is indicated'

Explanations must be tailored to the language skills and apparent educational attainment of the patient. Use by the patient of the doctor's technical language (for example an expression like 'cognitive deficit' or even a word as apparently

---

1   Good Medical Practice (GMC) https://www.gmc-uk.org/guidance/good_medical_practice/communicate_effectively.asp

2   http://www.aomrc.org.uk/wp-content/uploads/2018/09/Please_write_to_me_Guidance_010918.pdf

straightforward as 'chronic') may not reflect a real understanding of its meaning either generally or specifically in the patient's case.

The healthcare professional should develop simple everyday language explanations for all of those matters which need to be regularly addressed with patients, and, while remaining sensitive to the patient, give the patient an honest and complete picture.

> ### DEVELOP SIMPLE EXPLANATIONS FOR MATTERS REGULARLY ADDRESSED WITH PATIENTS

The guidance of the Academy of Medical Royal Colleges referred to above advises, and explains the advantage in communication terms of, writing outpatient clinic letters directly to patients with a copy being sent to the patient's GP, rather than the other way round. It should be more natural to write of a patient in the second person (you) rather than in the third person (she or her). But it should also become more informative, supportive and useful.

- It should strengthen the doctor-patient relationship
- It should better act as a reminder of important information given at the consultation
- It is more useful for the patient when it comes to sharing the information as to what was said by the clinician with family or carers
- It better equips the patient to share the information with other healthcare providers
- The patient is better able to point out any errors in the contents of the letter
- The GP is more readily able to understand what the consultant is writing, and will spend less time explaining to patients what the letter means.

However particularly in relation to the last bullet point above, it is also important that the precision of language needed to communicate to a medically qualified person significant information is not lost through over-simplification.

9.2   Patients' families

The same issues referred to in the last section above in relation to patients apply equally in relation to the patient's family members or other supporters. Miscommunication leads to misunderstanding which often leads to litigation or complaints.

Different family members may have different levels of understanding or may have different levels of emotional involvement and this must, so far as is possible, be catered for. It is normally possible to identify a 'family dynamic' when meeting with family members, and this should be used to adjust or vary the way in which information is communicated. It is not just the patient, or it is not just the patient's partner, parent or child who should be communicated with, but all of those present. Providing the opportunity for questions or for a request for further explanations from all of those whose presence is consented to by the patient is important.

9.3 Professionals

No issue should arise in communicating with other healthcare professionals, and in particular with those with expertise in the same field. Nonetheless it is important to allow for the opportunity for questions or for a request for further explanations from other healthcare professionals. Hierarchical issues may arise, resulting in a difficulty in challenging or questioning communications, or in seeking greater explanation or clarification, from those of greater experience or higher standing in the organisation by those lower down, or perhaps perceiving themselves as lower down, the scale. It may also result in the impression of a dismissive approach by the more senior to the observations, opinions or questions of the junior. (See also the observations of the AoMRC about consultants communicating with GPs referred to in Section 9.1 above.)

Communicating with lawyers, particularly in the context of litigation or professional complaints, should be predicated on much the same basis as communicating with patients. No assumptions should be made as to the lawyer's understanding of matters relevant to the doctor's expertise, and all except the most basic technical language should be used only on the basis that it needs to be explained.

Lawyers use logic and therefore seek logic in explanations provided to them. A doctor's opinion on a matter can be understood, without understanding of the underlying medicine, if the doctor identifies the material facts (or factors), and explains the reasoning process that leads to the conclusion or opinion (as explained above in Section 8.5 in relation to making medical records). In addressing why another doctor was wrong in a conclusion or opinion, it should then be straightforward to identify the material facts not taken into account by that doctor, or the immateriality of facts she has taken into account, or the errors in the reasoning process.

In addition to using logic, lawyers use language very precisely and consistently. It is therefore important for a doctor to do the same. This is most apparent when considering the legal tests that the law imposes, such as proof on the balance of probabilities, in which 'may be', 'should be', 'possibly' all have meanings significantly different to 'probably', which means 'more likely than not'; or such as applying the Bolam test in an opinion on clinical negligence (see Section 15.5(i) below).

To tell a lawyer that a patient is 'better' could mean that there has been an improvement (a comparative situation) but could mean that the patient has recovered. To say that symptoms will not resolve 'in the foreseeable future' leaves wholly unresolved what period is being talked about, although the lawyer is most probably thinking of a much longer period than the doctor.

> COMMUNICATE IN A MANNER YOUR AUDIENCE
> WILL UNDERSTAND
>
> UNDERSTAND YOUR AUDIENCE BEFORE YOU TRY
> TO COMMUNICATE

9.4   The media

It is most unlikely to be advisable to speak to the media before taking advice, particularly if it is about possible or ongoing litigation or investigations. In any event, a response to a query should be carefully considered and prepared.

Responding to matters raised on social media, where matters can rapidly spiral out of control, requires an even greater degree of care (and restraint).

Obviously, you must protect patient confidentiality, and even with the express consent of a patient should take great care before discussing matters in public.

Your professional indemnity body is probably the first point of contact if you are the subject of media interest. Your professional association, trade union, and College or Faculty are also good sources of advice.

Where media interest relates to NHS practice, then this situation is likely to be covered by your contract and you should refer the matter to your employer before any response is made.

Useful references

Please, write to me. Writing outpatient clinic letters to patients. Guidance (AoMRC)[3]

Handling the Media – a guide for doctors (MDU)[4]

Confidentiality: responding to criticism in the media (GMC)[5]

---

3   http://www.aomrc.org.uk/wp-content/uploads/2018/09/Please_write_to_me_Guid-ance_010918.pdf

4   https://www.medicalprotection.org/docs/default-source/pdfs/uk-media-centre/handling-the-media-guide.pdf?sfvrsn=8

5   https://www.gmc-uk.org/-/media/documents/confidentiality---responding-to-criticism-in-the-media_pdf-70062408.pdf

10

Confidentiality

You must treat information about patients as confidential. This includes after a patient has died. (Good Medical Practice (GMC) para 50)

Chapter outline

The concept of treating information about a patient as confidential is well understood. What is less well understood is when disclosure can properly be made. This Chapter looks at disclosure with the patient's express and implied consent, the circumstances when disclosure may be in a patient's best interest, or may be required by law, or may be in the public interest, and the importance of recording the justification for such disclosure.

The law also imposes duties on a clinician and the healthcare provider organisation in relation to data protection and this Chapter considers some of the implications of those duties. Reflective practice is an essential part of professional development but as this section will indicate, this should, and can, still respect the patient's confidentiality.

10.1 Patient's confidence

Confidential medical care is recognised in law as being in the public interest. The fact that people are encouraged to seek advice and treatment knowing that information provided will be treated as confidential benefits society as a whole as well as the individual.

Doctors are under ethical and legal duties to protect patients' personal information from improper disclosure, but it is necessary for the safe and effective care of patients for information to be shared appropriately. In addition, medical research, service planning and financial audit need patient information. Finally, disclosure may be necessary for reasons of public protection.

Whenever in doubt, the legal and ethical basis for any disclosure should be considered and checked. The GMC provides useful guidance in *Confidentiality: good practice in handling patient information*[1].

Disclosure in response to police inquiries is considered in greater detail in Section 11.2 below.

A patient's personal information may be disclosed without breaching duties of confidentiality when any of the following circumstances applies.

(i)   Disclosure with the patient's consent

The patient's consent may be express and may be given orally (as well as in writing) but it may also be implied or implicit, for example where it is necessary for the patient's own care, the information is necessary to support the patient's direct care, and the person with whom it is shared understands that it is given to them in confidence. These are circumstances when it is reasonable to infer that the patient agrees to the sharing of the information. If for any reason it is thought that the patient would be surprised to learn that the information is being disclosed, then express consent should be sought and, of course, recorded.

Implied consent can also be relied on where the information is needed for local clinical audit, although it may in those circumstances be possible to provide anonymised information. In this regard it should be noted that simply removing the patient's name, age, address or other personal identifiers is not sufficient. In addition, post codes, patient's initials, NHS number, National Insurance number and key dates may also identify the person concerned. The Information Commissioner's Office code should be consulted for further advice[2].

---

1   https://www.gmc-uk.org/-/media/documents/Confidentiality_good_practice_in_ handling_patient_information___English_0417.pdf_70080105.pdf

2   Anonymisation: managing data protection risk code of practice ICO (2012)

(ii)   The disclosure is in a patient's best interest

Where a patient is found to lack mental capacity, a decision about disclosure of confidential information can be made on the basis of the patient's best interests. (Mental capacity is considered in Chapter 14.) Personal information can still be disclosed if it is for the overall benefit of the patient.

The patient should, where appropriate, be involved in the decision to disclose confidential information. In deciding whether or not to disclose the information, consideration should be given to what is known about the patient's previously expressed preferences. To this end the views as to the patient's preferences, feelings or beliefs of anyone with legal authority to act on the patient's behalf or who has been appointed to represent them, or of anyone close to the patient and of anyone in the healthcare team, should be obtained. It might be appropriate to share some information with the patient's relatives, friends or carers in order to be able to assess the best interests of the patient.

As the decision in relation to someone lacking capacity is made on the basis of their best interests, should the patient who is found to lack capacity ask that information is not disclosed, and cannot be persuaded otherwise, then the information should nonetheless be disclosed to an appropriate person if that is considered to be in the patient's best interests.

Particular care is necessary when the question arises as to disclosing information about children who may be at risk, and the GMC's guidance *Protecting children and young people: the responsibilities of doctors* should be consulted[3]. If, for example, parents refuse to permit disclosure of information about a child to the police, then a decision must be made in the best interests of the child. An appropriate agency (local authority children's services, the NSPCC or the police) should be informed promptly if there are concerns that a child or young person is at risk of, or is suffering, abuse or neglect unless it is not in their best interests to do so. Concerns, not certainty, are sufficient because the possible consequences of not sharing relevant information will generally outweigh any harm that sharing the concerns with an appropriate agency might cause.

(iii)   The disclosure is required by law

Disclosure is required by law in a number of instances, such as the notification of infectious diseases, the provision of health and social care services, the prevention of terrorism, the investigation of road accidents and suspicion of FGM[4]. Once the clinician is satisfied that disclosure is required by law, and also, and importantly, what information must be disclosed, the patient should normally be informed that disclosure will be made unless telling the patient would undermine the purpose of the disclosure, for example by prejudicing the prevention,

---

3   https://www.gmc-uk.org/static/documents/content/Protecting_children_and_young_people_-_English_1015.pdf

4   See Chapter 11 below for examples of disclosure required to be made to the police

detection or prosecution of serious crime.

Disclosure must also be made if ordered by a judge or presiding officer of a court, but only the information required by the court should be disclosed. Again, the patient should be informed of the information that will be disclosed unless doing so would undermine the purpose of the disclosure.

The clinician may disclose the information to a legal adviser without the consent of the patient in order to get advice as to its disclosure.

There are statutory arrangements in place for considering whether disclosing personal information without consent would benefit patients or the public sufficiently to outweigh a patient's right to privacy in certain limited cases, such as for medical research or the management of health or social care services[5].

(iv)   The disclosure is in the public interest

There can be a public interest in disclosing confidential information if the benefits to an individual or society outweigh both the public and the patient's interest in keeping the information confidential. For that reason, disclosure may be justified to protect individuals or society from risks of serious harm, such as from serious communicable diseases or serious crime, or to prevent serious harm or abuse such as child abuse or neglect[6].

'Serious crime' is not formally defined but will include crimes that cause serious physical or psychological harm to individuals (such as murder, manslaughter, rape and child abuse); and crimes that cause serious harm to the security of the state and public order; and 'crimes that involve substantial financial gain or loss' are also mentioned in the same category[7]. A minor assault, or one causing only 'actual bodily harm' but not 'wounding' or 'grievous bodily harm' (see Section 15.6(iii)), would not come within this category and, subject to the following paragraph, consent will be required before disclosing confidential information.

The GMC guidance referred to above (*Confidentiality: good practice in handling patient information*) provides other examples where disclosure may be in the public interest. When victims of violence refuse police assistance, disclosure may still be justified if others remain at risk, for example from someone who is prepared to use weapons, or from domestic violence when children or others may be at risk. Other examples include where a risk of death or serious harm to others might arise, as when a patient is not fit to drive[8], or has been diagnosed

---

5   Section 251 of the National Health Service Act 2006 (This provision does not apply in Scotland.)

6   See Chapter 11 below for examples of disclosure required to be made to the police

7   Confidentiality: NHS Code of Practice Supplementary Guidance: Public Interest Disclosures (Department of Health, 2003)

8   Confidentiality: patients' fitness to drive and reporting concerns to the DVLA or DVA (GMC)

with a serious communicable disease[9], or poses a serious risk to others through being unfit for work[10].

A decision to disclose in such a case is a balancing exercise, weighing up:

- the potential harm or distress to the patient arising from the disclosure – for example, in terms of their future engagement with treatment and their overall health
- the potential harm to trust in doctors generally – for example, if it is widely perceived that doctors will readily disclose information about patients without consent
- the potential harm to others (whether to a specific person or people, or to the public more broadly) if the information is not disclosed
- the potential benefits to an individual or to society arising from the release of the information
- the nature of the information to be disclosed, and any views expressed by the patient
- whether the harms can be avoided or benefits gained without breaching the patient's privacy or, if not, what is the minimum intrusion[11].

(v)   Recording decisions

The importance of recording the decision made in all of these cases involving a decision to disclose confidential information, and the reasons for such decision, should be apparent. Where there is guidance as to the considerations to be taken into account in making such a decision, as from the GMC and referred to in this section, then the recorded reasoning should set out briefly all of those consider-ations applicable to the particular patient. (For 'Records and making notes' see Chapter 8 above.)

10.2 Data protection

It is essential to ensure that any personal information is held securely and protected from improper access or disclosure, and from loss. Substantial financial penalties can be imposed for failures to do so. Whenever practical the minimum of necessary personal information should be used.

The General Data Protection Regulations came into force in May 2018. These introduced specific legal requirements concerning consent, transmission, and storage of personal data which affect anyone including doctors who processes such data. For the purposes of the Regulations 'personal data' is information that relates to an identified or identifiable individual. Persons may be identifiable directly, by their name or initials, or indirectly, by reference to a number or some

---

9   Confidentiality: disclosing information about serious communicable diseases

10   Confidentiality: disclosing information for employment, insurance and similar purposes (GMC

11   Confidentiality: good practice in handling patient information (GMC) para 68

other identifying factor or a number of factors.

Processing of such personal data, that is any use of it, is lawful only if one of 6 criteria is fulfilled:

- The data subject, in this case the patient, has given consent to the processing of his or her personal data for one or more specific purposes
- Processing is necessary for the performance of a contract to which the data subject is party or to take steps at the request of the data subject prior to entering into a contract (unlikely to apply in an NHS context)
- Processing is necessary for compliance with a legal obligation to which the data controller, in this case the healthcare provider, is subject
- Processing is necessary to protect the vital interests of the data subject or of another person
- Processing is necessary for the performance of a task carried out in the public interest or in the exercise of official authority vested in the data controller
- Processing is necessary for the purposes of the legitimate interests pursued by the data controller or by a third party, except where such interests are overridden by the interests or fundamental rights and freedoms of the data subject (this condition does not apply to processing carried out by public authorities in the performance of their tasks).

Patients are entitled to request access to, the location of, the amendment to, and the erasure of their data. This requires knowledge by the data controller of the location of the personal data and all copies of it. There is a requirement of both transparency and accountability in the handling of personal data.

The security and privacy of personal information must be ensured at all times, including when the information is being passed, with the patient's consent, from one medical practitioner to another, and whether in paper or electronic form.

It is therefore essential to physically protect both paper and electronic records and notes from unauthorised access. To leave papers absentmindedly in the canteen or washroom, or to have records or images on a laptop or mobile phone which is stolen from a car if the device is not properly password protected and encrypted, are potentially serious breaches of the data protection legislation.

If images are shared for teaching or research purposes, then it is essential that they are anonymised, that is that all personal identifiers that might lead to the identification of the person either directly or indirectly are removed. Consent is not required for use of anonymised pictures and images for teaching or research purposes (see *Making and using visual and audio recordings of patients* (GMC)[12]). The Information Commissioner's Office has provided guidance on anonymising

---

12   https://www.gmc-uk.org/-/media/documents/making-and-using-visual-and-audio-record-ings-of-patients_pdf-58838365.pdf

data[13]. See also *Confidentiality: disclosing information for education and training purposes* (GMC)[14] and *Guidance on the use of patient images obtained as part of standard care for teaching, training and research* (Royal College of Radiologists)[15].

10.3 Reflective practice

Doctors are required to reflect on their performance and professional value on a regular basis, and the importance of this is reflected in guidance to all healthcare professionals[16]. It is important that these are written openly and honestly, otherwise their purpose will be undermined. However, to protect patient confidentiality these should be anonymised so far as is possible. There should be no patient identifiable information contained within written reflections. (See Section 10.1(i) above and the following paragraphs for further consideration of anonymity.)

The Academy of Medical Royal Colleges issued *Guidance for entering information onto e-portfolios* in October 2016 specifically in relation to trainees, and this has general application for all reflective practice. In the light of concerns arising out of the gross negligence manslaughter trial of Dr Bawa-Garba[17] interim guidance was produced in March 2018 pending the production of further definitive guidance by AoMRC with the GMC and other bodies. This is an evolving area in which further written guidance is therefore expected.

> REFLECTIVE NOTES MUST BE ANNONYMISED

It is important to understand that notes in reflective practice are not medical records, but are part of the doctor's educational process. Nonetheless information in such reflective records may have to be disclosed to third parties without the consent of the data subject (the patient), to:

- A party to court proceedings or a coroner in response to a court order to that effect
- The police for crime prevention purposes.

In addition, they may have to be released to a patient in response to a patient subject access request if they amount to personal data and are identifiable as relating to the patient. In relation to fitness to practise investigations, the GMC has stated that it will not seek disclosure of such reflections (see for example this

13   https://ico.org.uk/media/for-organisations/documents/1061/anonymisation-code.pdf

14   https://www.gmc-uk.org/-/media/documents/Confidentiality___Disclosing_information_for_education_and_training_purposes.pdf_70063667.pdf

15   https://www.rcr.ac.uk/system/files/publication/field_publication_files/bfcr177_use_of_pateint_images.pdf

16   See for example the NMC's Standards to support learning and assessment in practice

17   https://www.bailii.org/ew/cases/EWCA/Civ/2018/1879.html

reference[18]), although practitioners might choose to disclose their reflections to demonstrate 'insight' in the course of an investigation.

The original advice from AoMRC is to keep reflective notes as fully anonymised as possible, avoiding providing information that might identify practitioners, patients, parents and staff. Sometimes it is impossible to avoid providing information from which a patient can be identified, but this should be minimised. Sometimes the facts referred to are so unusual as to be readily identifiable to those familiar with a particular case. The *Guidance* gives suggestions as to how the notes should be worded to this end while remaining a useful educational tool.

The October 2016 AoMRC advice states:

> *Data that may be considered personal data could be [the patient's] initials combined with their religion and unique characteristic of their health condition. Doctors should be advised that they should avoid referring to names (by referring to patient instead as X), dates of births (they can instead refer to the patient's approximate age if necessary), addresses, or any unique condition or circumstance of that patient which may allow someone to identify the patient when used in conjunction with other information they have access to. There may be the occasional case when the identity of the patient is recognisable by the unique set of circumstances but the possibility of identification should be reduced as much as possible.*

It is important to recognise that the combination of data may identify the patient to which the reflections relate. Although reflections are commonly written shortly after the event to which they relate, thereby making them more readily referable to a particular incident, they can be entered on the e-portfolio at a later time, thereby further anonymising the entry.

The AoMRC interim guidance suggests that if reflections focus specifically on reactions to and learning from an incident, developing insight and identifying improvements in practice, then the risk of the reflections being disclosable in proceedings is reduced. Reflective statements need therefore to focus on the learning extracted from significant events. They should not be a full discussion of the case or situation.

It should be noted that although much of the recent concern about the potential use of reflective practice arose out of the trial of Dr Bawa-Garba, her reflections were not before the jury at the trial and the jury was told to disregard any remarks documented after the events to which they related[19].

---

18 https://www.bma.org.uk/collective-voice/influence/key-negotiations/training-and-work-force/the-case-of-dr-bawa-garba/reflective-practice

19 http://www.pulsetoday.co.uk/news/gp-topics/legal/revealed-how-reflections-were-used-in-the-bawa-garba-case/20036090.articleh

Further reading

Anonymisation: managing data protection risk code of practice ICO (2012)[20]

Confidentiality: good practice in handling patient information (GMC)[21]

Confidentiality and health records tool kit (BMA)[22]

Protecting children and young people: the responsibilities of doctors (GMC)[23]

Confidentiality: Patients' fitness to drive and reporting concerns to the DVLA or DVA (GMC)[24]

Confidentiality: Disclosing information about serious communicable diseases (GMC)[25]

Confidentiality: Disclosing information for employment, insurance and similar purposes (GMC)[26]

Confidentiality: Disclosing information for education and training purposes (GMC)[27]

Confidentiality: Reporting gunshot and knife wounds (GMC)[28]

General Data Protection Regulations Guidance (NHS Digital)[29]

Confidentiality: NHS Code of Practice (November 2003)[30]

---

20   https://ico.org.uk/media/for-organisations/documents/1061/anonymisation-code.pdf

21   https://www.gmc-uk.org/static/documents/content/Confidentiality_good_practice_in_
     handling_patient_information_-_English_0417.pdf

22   https://www.bma.org.uk/advice/employment/ethics/confidentiality-and-health-records

23   https://www.gmc-uk.org/static/documents/content/Protecting_children_and_young_
     people_-_English_1015.pdf

24   https://www.gmc-uk.org/-/media/documents/confidentiality---patients-fitness-to-drive-
     and-reporting-concerns-to-dvla-or-dva_pdf-70063275.pdf

25   https://www.gmc-uk.org/-/media/documents/confidentiality---disclosing-information-
     about-serious-communicable-diseases_pdf-70061396.pdf

26   https://www.gmc-uk.org/-/media/documents/confidentiality---disclosing-information-for-
     employment--insurance-and-similar-purposes_pdf-70064157.pdf

27   https://www.gmc-uk.org/-/media/documents/Confidentiality___Disclosing_informa-
     tion_for_education_and_training_purposes.pdf_70063667.pdf

28   https://www.gmc-uk.org/-/media/documents/Confidentiality___Reporting_gunshot_
     and_knife_wounds.pdf_70063779.pdf

29   https://digital.nhs.uk/information-governance-alliance/General-Data-Protection-Regula-
     tion-guidance

30   https://assets.publishing.service.gov.uk/government/uploads/system/uploads/attachment_
     data/file/200146/Confidentiality_-_NHS_Code_of_Practice.pdf

Confidentiality: NHS Code of Practice Supplementary Guidance: Public Interest Disclosures (November 2010)[31]

Guidance for entering information into e-portfolios (AoMRC) October 2016[32]

Interim guidance on reflective practice (AoMRC) March 2018[33]

31   https://assets.publishing.service.gov.uk/government/uploads/system/uploads/attachment_data/file/216476/dh_122031.pdf

32   http://www.aomrc.org.uk/wp-content/uploads/2016/11/Academy_Guidance_on_e-Portfo-lios_201916-5.pdf

33   http://www.aomrc.org.uk/wp-content/uploads/2018/03/Interim-guidance-on-reflective-practice.pdf

11

Assisting the police with their inquiries

Chapter outline

Inquiries from the police of a clinician may be as a result of a complaint by someone about the clinician (most probably a patient or a patient's family) or may relate to inquiries by the police into someone else in relation to which it is thought that the clinician may be able to provide relevant evidence. This Chapter will consider both of these two kinds of inquiries and the issues which arise if the clinician is approached by the police to provide information.

This Chapter will consider the situation which might arise for the clinician treating patients involved in road traffic incidents and possible terrorism offences, or suffering gunshot and knife wounds or female genital mutilation, or involved in other serious crimes, the seizure of evidence by the police and the provision of witness statements by the clinician.

11.1 Complaint about the clinician being questioned

It may be that a patient has misunderstood the actions of a clinician or the purpose of a consultation or that something has gone seriously wrong. But whatever circumstances the complaint might arise out of, the clinician is almost certainly into new territory and outside her comfort zone when approached by the police and it is essential to obtain legal advice before being questioned. The medical protection organisation is most probably the first point of urgent contact, failing which a solicitor with experience in representing clinicians.

Without knowing what it is that the police are investigating in some detail, which will put the events in the appropriate context, it is difficult to provide useful and appropriate answers to questions, and, so far as it is required to do so, with proper regard for the confidentiality of the patient. In any event, there is no obligation to provide a statement, whether oral or written, to the police.

The police are required to caution a person before interviewing them if it is suspected that they have committed an offence. If questions are commenced on the basis that a person is likely to be a prosecution witness but it appears in fact that the person may have committed an offence, then at that point a caution is required before further questions are asked. The caution is as follows:

> You do not have to say anything. But it may harm your defence if you do not mention when questioned something which you later rely on in Court. Anything you do say may be given in evidence.

Therefore, while informing the suspect that she does not have to say anything, it also warns her that anything she says may be used in evidence and that should she fail to mention something which she later relies on in her defence, then that is a matter which can be brought to the court's attention and could harm her case.

The police do not have to arrest someone before interviewing them. The interview can still take place at a police station but it can also take place at the suspect's home or place of work. If invited to voluntarily accompany the police to the police station, then it is best to politely decline until such time as legal advice has been obtained. If having attended the police station the suspect wishes to leave, then the suspect is free to do so at any time unless the police have grounds to, and do, arrest the individual.

Should questioning take place nonetheless without the clinician having obtained legal advice, then it is usually advisable to exercise the right to silence politely and to decline to answer questions until the clinician has had the opportunity to speak with a lawyer. The lawyer will ensure that the police are entitled to question the clinician and will ensure that the procedures are followed, including the disclosure of information prior to the commencement of any interview, so that the nature of the criticism being made against the clinician and the context of the questions is known before the questions are answered.

11.2 Inquiries into somone other than the clinician

Clinicians may be asked to provide information about someone else and about events in which they have been involved. This gives rise to issues as to when the personal information can be given despite the patient's expectation of confidentiality. This section must therefore be read together with Chapter 10 above 'Confidentiality'.

Assuming that the patient has provided consent, then a witness statement should be provided promptly to assist the police in their inquiries. The situation where the patient does not give consent or where it is considered inappropriate to ask the patient for consent requires careful consideration.

The GMC guidance *Confidentiality: good practice in handling patient information*[1] states:

> 1. *Trust is an essential part of the doctor patient relationship and confidentiality is central to this. Patients may avoid seeking medical help, or may under-report symptoms, if they think that their personal information will be disclosed by doctors without consent, or without the chance to have some control over the timing or amount of information shared.*
>
> 60. *Doctors owe a duty of confidentiality to their patients, but they also have a wider duty to protect and promote the health of patients and the public.*
>
> 62. *You should ask for a patient's consent to disclose information for the protection of others unless the information is required by law or it is not safe, appropriate or practicable to do so. You should consider any reasons given for refusal.*
>
> 64. *If it is not practicable or appropriate to seek consent, and in exceptional cases where a patient has refused consent, disclosing personal information may be justified in the public interest if failure to do so may expose others to a risk of death or serious harm. The benefits to an individual or to society of the disclosure must outweigh both the patient's and the public interest in keeping the information confidential.*
>
> 67. *Before deciding whether disclosure would be justified in the public interest you should consider whether it is practicable or appropriate to seek consent (see paragraph 14). You should not ask for consent if you have already decided to disclose information in the public interest but you should tell the patient about your intention to disclose personal information, unless it is not safe or practicable to do so. If the patient objects to the disclosure you should consider any reasons they give for objecting.*

---

1   https://www.gmc-uk.org/ethical-guidance/ethical-guidance-for-doctors/confidentiality/ethical-and-legal-duties-of-confidentiality

68. When deciding whether the public interest in disclosing information outweighs the patient's and the public interest in keeping the information confidential, you must consider:

a. the potential harm or distress to the patient arising from the disclosure – for example, in terms of their future engagement with treatment and their overall health

b. the potential harm to trust in doctors generally – for example, if it is widely perceived that doctors will readily disclose information about patients without consent

c. the potential harm to others (whether to a specific person or people, or to the public more broadly) if the information is not disclosed

d. the potential benefits to an individual or to society arising from the release of the information

e. the nature of the information to be disclosed, and any views expressed by the patient

f. whether the harms can be avoided or benefits gained without breaching the patient's privacy or, if not, what is the minimum intrusion.

If you consider that failure to disclose the information would leave individuals or society exposed to a risk so serious that it outweighs the patient's and the public interest in maintaining confidentiality, you should disclose relevant information promptly to an appropriate person or authority.

(i)　Road traffic

A person shall, if required, *'give any information which it is in his power to give and may lead to identification of the driver'* of a vehicle alleged to be guilty of an offence[2]. Failure to provide this information is a criminal offence. Therefore if a driver suspected of a road traffic offence seeks treatment, the police can, for example, ask for their name and address but the provision does not require (and therefore permit) the giving of information about injuries sustained or the giving of information about any other person who may have been with the alleged driver.

(ii)　Terrorism

Under Section 38B of the Terrorism Act 2000[3] everyone (including doctors) must tell the police if they become aware of information that they believe would help

---

2　Section 172(2) Road Traffic Act 1988. The provision applies also in Scotland but not in Northern Ireland

3　This provision applies also in Scotland and Northern Ireland

prevent a terrorist act or secure the arrest or prosecution of someone involved in terrorism. Information must be disclosed which might be of material assistance in preventing an act of terrorism or securing the arrest of someone for a terrorist offence. Failure to do so without reasonable excuse is a criminal offence. What might amount to a reasonable excuse is not defined in the Act but it is difficult to envisage the situation arising in the clinical context which would amount to such an excuse.

(iii)   Gunshot and knife wounds

Where a patient has sustained gunshot or knife wounds, disclosure of information including confidential information will normally be appropriate on the basis of 'public interest' (see Section 10.1(iv) above). GMC guidance is clear that the police should usually be informed whenever a person presents with a gunshot wound. Even accidental shootings involving lawfully held guns raise serious issues for the police, such as in relation to firearms' licensing. The police should also usually be informed when a person presents with a wound from an attack with a knife, blade or other sharp instrument. The initial information need not include name or address.

However the police should not usually be informed if a knife or blade injury appears to be accidental, or a result of self-harm. There may also be other circumstances in which contacting the police is not considered proportionate. For example, this might be the case if it is considered that no one other than the patient is at risk of harm, and that contacting the police might cause the patient harm or distress, or might damage the patient's trust in the treating doctor or doctors generally.

Treatment comes first, and therefore when the police arrive, they should not be allowed access to the patient if this would delay or hamper treatment or compromise the patient's recovery.

If the patient's treatment and condition permit the patient to speak to the police, then a member of the healthcare team should ask the patient whether she is willing to do so. If she is not, then the healthcare team and the police must abide by the patient's decision.

(iv)   Investigations in relation to other serious crimes

In relation to police investigations into other serious crimes, confidential information should be provided if disclosure is in the public interest. Therefore if it is considered that failure to disclose the information would leave individuals or society exposed to a risk so serious that it outweighs the patient's and the public interest in maintaining confidentiality, relevant information should be disclosed promptly to an appropriate person or authority (see paras 67 and 68 of the GMC Guidance set out above).

(v)   Police searching for a missing person

Police may seek information as to whether a named person is in the hospital. In the absence of the patient's consent, or, in relation to a person without capacity, a decision in their best interests, or unless disclosure is in the public interest (to prevent serious harm or death to the patient or another person), or unless disclosure is ordered by a court, there are no grounds for releasing such information about an adult.

In relation to questions about the possible location of a child or young person under 18, then the information should be disclosed to the police, even if there are good reasons for not informing members of the child's family (which reasons should be shared with the police).

(vi)   Female genital mutilation

All health and social care professionals who discover that an act of FGM appears to have been carried out on a girl under 18 years old must report it to the police[4]. The duty to report is on that professional. Such a duty may arise where the girl informs the person that an act of FGM (however described) has been carried out on her and also where physical signs are observed on the girl appearing to show that an act of FGM has been carried out on her, unless there is reason to believe that the act was, or was part of, a surgical operation for health purposes or connected with labour or birth.

Such disclosure does not breach any obligation of confidentiality.

Home Office guidance[5] recommends that in line with safeguarding best practice, the girl and/or her parents or guardians should be contacted to explain the report, why it is being made, and what it means. Wherever possible, this discussion should take place in advance of, or in parallel to, the report being made. However, if informing the child or her parents or guardians about the report might result in a risk of serious harm to the child or anyone else, or of the family fleeing the country, then the report should not be discussed.

(vii)   Seizure of evidence

The police may seize evidence, such as clothing, relevant to their inquiries, that is if they have reasonable grounds for believing that it is evidence in relation to an offence and it is necessary to seize it in order to prevent the evidence being concealed, lost, altered or destroyed[6].

---

4   Section 5B Female Genital Mutilation Act 2003. This provision applies to England and Wales only.

5   *Mandatory Reporting of Female Genital Mutilation – procedural information*

6   Section 19(3) Police and Criminal Evidence Act 1984. This provision applies to England and Wales only

(viii)   Witness statements

Assuming that patient confidentiality does not prevent the making of a witness statement, a witness statement is used to provide the evidence of relevant facts to the court. It is common to be asked to provide a witness statement about injuries for which a person has been treated and which are suspected to be the result of an assault. Frequently a witness statement is used in place of the clinician having to attend court to give that evidence, and the statement therefore has a declaration confirming the truth of the statement and acknowledging that if it is knowingly false then the maker can be prosecuted for perjury.

The statement should be written in such a way that it can be readily understood by a lay person and therefore where medical terms are used, they should be explained. It should not include opinion or speculation, but should be limited to factual information only.

On occasions, such statements are required as a matter of urgency to enable the police to investigate a serious crime, in which case a further opportunity to consider the witness statement should subsequently be provided. However it is important, for practical reasons and because of the nature of the declaration signed by the clinician, that the witness statement is accurate, truthful and reliable.

The form and content of such a statement is considered in Chapter 6 'Preparing a witness statement' above.

Further reading

Ethical and legal duties of confidentiality GMC[7]

Confidentiality: Reporting gunshot and knife wounds (GMC)[8]

A universal FGM flowchart and reporting tool (RCEM) June 2017[9]

Mandatory Reporting of Female Genital Mutilation – procedural information (Home Office)[10]

Providing a Witness Statement for the Police RCEM (February 2012)[11]

---

7   https://www.gmc-uk.org/ethical-guidance/ethical-guidance-for-doctors/confidentiality/
     ethical-and-legal-duties-of-confidentiality

8   https://www.gmc-uk.org/-/media/documents/Confidentiality___Reporting_gunshot_
     and_knife_wounds.pdf_70063779.pdf

9   https://www.rcem.ac.uk/docs/RCEM Guidance/FGM - BP Guide - Jul 2017.pdf

10   https://assets.publishing.service.gov.uk/government/uploads/system/uploads/attachment_
     data/file/573782/FGM_Mandatory_Reporting_-_procedural_information_nov16_FINAL.
     pdf

11   https://www.rcem.ac.uk/docs/College Guidelines/5z15. Providing a witness statement for
     the Police (Feb 2012).pdf

12

Patients in custody

12.1   Patients accompanied by the police
12.2   Patients from prison

Chapter outline

Issues can arise for the clinician treating patients who are under arrest or who arrive from places of detention, with the police or with prison staff. This Chapter considers the issues that commonly arise in such situations and how to approach the conflicts that may arise between the state's interest in securing the prisoner and the clinician's interest in treating the patient.

12.1 Patients accompanied by the police

A patient who is brought into hospital by the police, and who is under arrest and therefore in their custody, is entitled to exactly the same standard of care as all other patients. The clinician's duty in relation to consent and confidentiality is exactly as for all patients.

Such a patient may have been brought from police custody at a police station because of concern that has arisen during detention over health issues or may have been detained elsewhere and is being brought to the hospital because of concern for health before being taken to a police station. It is not the role of a hospital, but of an appropriate healthcare professional at the police station, to decide whether a person is fit to be detained by police, and that is the case even if the police are experiencing a delay in obtaining the attendance of an appropriate HCP.

The RCEM Best Practice Guideline *Emergency Department Patients in Police Custody* (June 2016) suggests that the initial questions at hospital to be made to police officers, to help understand the situation better and assist in maintaining safety, should be:

1.   Which station are the police from and what are the contact details?

2.   Is the patient under arrest, held under Section 136[1] or simply being accompanied?

3.   Has the patient been searched?

Police officers must remain with such patients throughout their time in hospital. Where the patient is restrained (normally with handcuffs, and sometimes secured to one or even two police officers) then any decision about removal of restraints must be made by medical staff in collaboration with the police officers, who will only remove restraints if they consider it safe to do so. Reasons for refusal to remove restraints should be recorded in the medical notes.

A detained patient is entitled to the same confidentiality as any other patient[2] and should if possible be free to discuss medical matters with clinicians in confidence.

In the case of an arrested person, the patient may be willing to provide the clinical team with more relevant information when the police are out of hearing. However it may not always be possible to discuss medical matters in private with the patient. If the patient is actively aggressive or considered by the police to be potentially aggressive or otherwise requires to be restrained in the public interest, they will remain present. In other cases, police officers may consider it appropriate to be in sight but out of hearing, but if not, then any recording equipment they have (such as body cameras) should be turned off.

There may be circumstances where information provided by, or about, the patient, despite its confidential nature, should be disclosed because it is in the public interest to do so, as in the case of a patient with a serious communicable disease who may by her behaviour be putting others at risk (see Chapter 10 'Confidentiality' above).

---

1   See Section 14.5(3) below

2   See Chapter 10 above

Treatment will be as for any other patient and requires consent as for any other patient. A patient who has mental capacity may therefore refuse treatment. Where treatment is refused, the assessment of capacity should be recorded in the hospital notes and the risks of non-treatment must be spelt out to the patient and also recorded. The option of returning for treatment should be given and this also must be recorded in the hospital notes and in the documentation provided on discharge to police custody.

Medication required for treatment, along with written instructions for use, should be given to the patient, or if that is not possible, to the accompanying police officers.

Emergency Department staff treating a person in police custody do not have a role in taking evidence relevant to police inquiries, such as taking blood samples for toxicology levels, assessing and documenting injury for forensic purposes, undertaking sexual assault examinations or carrying out intimate body cavity searches. These are for appropriate police healthcare professionals. However clinical staff may quite properly be requested by the police to assist in preserving evidence, for example by setting aside clothing and placing it in bags provided by the police.

Patients will only be fit for discharge to police custody when they meet the usual discharge criteria for a patient to be safely discharged home. The assumption should be that there will be the minimum of clinical observation while in police custody. Facilities and provision will vary between police stations, and a telephone conversation with the custody officer may be necessary to clarify whether it is appropriate clinically to discharge a patient to the particular police station. The situation however is not comparable with a discharge home under the eyes and ears of a caring and attentive family member or friend.

When discharging a patient back to a police station it is important that along with the usual information as to diagnosis, treatment or medication, any requirements for observation are included, but it should also be appreciated that the opportunity for observation may be limited (which may render discharge inappropriate). Information provided to the police should be limited to that which is necessary to allow them to look after the patient whilst in custody unless the patient has given consent to disclosure and this has been recorded in the medical notes. This information must be provided in a manner that a lay individual can readily understand because there may be a delay before the patient can be reviewed by an appropriate healthcare professional at the police station. For example, in a head injury case, if it is considered appropriate to discharge, the information provided should include guidance as to circumstances which would give rise to further concern without any presumption that anyone responsible for the patient's care in the police station would have prior knowledge of what to look out for, or would understand medical terms.

If the patient does not consent to clinical information being given to the police, it can be provided in a sealed envelope for the attention of the healthcare professional and a copy should be retained on the hospital records. In addition, clinical staff at the custody suite should be contacted prior to the patient's discharge to discuss the patient's care and a note should be made of this conversation.

The RCEM guidance referred to above gives the difficult example of a violent and drunk patient who is too aggressive to remain in hospital but too drunk to be held safely in a cell. Such cases will require careful consideration and discussion between hospital clinicians and police custody officers to decide if discharge is appropriate.

Most Trusts will have a Discharge to Police Custody form to be completed prior to discharge.

If requests are made by the police for witness statements, this is unlikely to be so urgent that it cannot be dealt with in due course and therefore such statements should not be provided while working in an emergency department. (See Chapter 6 'Preparing a witness statement' above.)

12.2 Patients from prison

Prisoners are categorised according to the likelihood of their trying to escape using the following 4 categories of prisons in which they will be detained:

Category A: prisons holding individuals whose escape would be highly dangerous to the public or national security and therefore require conditions of maximum security.

Category B: prisons holding individuals who do not require maximum security, but for whom escape would still pose a large risk to members of the public.

Category C: prisons holding individuals who cannot be trusted in open conditions, but are unlikely to try to escape.

Category D: prisons holding individuals who can be reasonably trusted not to escape and are given the privilege of open conditions.

Hospitals may be seen by prison authorities as a security risk in which prisoners may try to give a false impression of their medical condition in order to attempt to escape.

The National Offender Management Service's *External Prisoner Movement Protocol* (2015) sets out the rules generally applicable so far as the escorting staff are concerned.

An assessment will have been made at the prison taking into account what is known about the prisoner, and the escorting staff will secure the prisoner in accordance with that assessment. Usually a prisoner will be handcuffed and a chain will connect the prisoner to a cuff on one of the escorting staff. If for clinical reasons a request is made to remove the restraint, and it should certainly be made if the restraint interferes with treatment, then the escorting staff will need to seek permission from their senior management team at the prison to do so, unless the situation has been covered in the prior assessment. In emergencies it may be necessary to insist on removal of restraints, in which case the escorting staff should comply. In any event handcuffs must be removed before use of a defibrillator.

Special rules apply in relation to pregnant women, who should not be handcuffed in active labour, or in other cases after arrival at hospital, unless there are indications that they may attempt to escape.

While the patient must be treated just as any other patient, similar issues arise in relation to confidentiality and privacy as with patients brought in by police officers (see the previous Section). The NOMS Protocol recognises a patient's right to privacy, where that is compatible with security issues, and makes clear that escorting staff who become aware of medical information about the prisoner during their stay in the hospital must treat it in confidence and should only record information which is relevant to the security of the escort.

Requests for information about a prisoner and messages passed to hospital staff for a prisoner must all be referred to the escorting staff and must not otherwise be responded to or passed on. Similarly visits can only take place if permission is granted by the prison and the escorting staff informed.

Care needs to be taken with any prescribed medication, which may be diverted for non-therapeutic use in a custodial setting, and discussion with the prison authority is required.

Further reading

Emergency Department Patients in Police Custody (RCEM June 2016)[3]

Supporting Nursing Staff Caring for Patients From Places of Detention (RCN)[4]

The National Offender Management Service's external prisoner movement protocol (2015)[5] (See in particular Section 6)

The medical role in restraint and control: custodial settings - Guidance from the British Medical Association (August 2009)[6]

---

3   https://www.rcem.ac.uk/docs/College Guidelines/5n. ED Patients in Police Custody (revised June 2016).pdf

4   https://www.rcn.org.uk/-/media/royal-college-of-nursing/documents/publications/2017/january/pub-005856.pdf

5   https://www.justice.gov.uk/downloads/offenders/psipso/psi-2015/psi-33-2015-external-prisoner-movement.pdf

6   https://www.bma.org.uk/-/media/files/pdfs/practical%20advice%20at%20work/ethics/medicalrolerestraintaug2009.pdf

13

Consenting

Chapter outline

This Chapter will look at consenting patients and the requirement to inform them about the risks of treatment options (and of no treatment). In the absence of any consent, the clinician may be guilty of battery and trespass, but in the absence of provision of adequate information, the clinician may be guilty of negligence and liable for damages following the decision in the case of *Montgomery*.

This Chapter will also look at some of the practicalities of obtaining appropriate consent – who should deal with it and when in relation to the treatment being discussed, what records should be kept, the nature of the discussion with the patient, the risks which need to be referred to, difficulties that may arise in communicating with patients, patients who do not want the information, and consenting children and young people.

13.1 General principles

Obtaining consent to treatment or investigations is a process of partnership between healthcare professional and patient, which involves:

1.   listening to patients and respecting their views about their health;

2.   discussing with patients what their diagnosis, prognosis, treatment and care involve;

3.   sharing with patients the information they want or need in order to make decisions;

4.   maximising patients' opportunities, and their ability, to make decisions for themselves;

5.   respecting patients' decisions.[1]

So long as a patient has capacity to make decisions for herself, the process should involve:

> *a) The doctor and patient make an assessment of the patient's condition, taking into account the patient's medical history, views, experience and knowledge.*
>
> *b) The doctor uses specialist knowledge and experience and clinical judgement, and the patient's views and understanding of their condition, to identify which investigations or treatments are likely to result in overall benefit for the patient. The doctor explains the options to the patient, setting out the potential benefits, risks, burdens and side effects of each option, including the option to have no treatment. The doctor may recommend a particular option which they believe to be best for the patient, but they must not put pressure on the patient to accept their advice.*
>
> *c) The patient weighs up the potential benefits, risks and burdens of the various options as well as any non-clinical issues that are relevant to them. The patient decides whether to accept any of the options and, if so, which one. They also have the right to accept or refuse an option for a reason that may seem irrational to the doctor, or for no reason at all[2].*

It may happen that a patient seeks treatment which the doctor considers inappropriate:

> *d) If the patient asks for a treatment that the doctor considers would not be of overall benefit to them, the doctor should discuss the issues with the patient*

---

1   Consent: patients and doctors working together (GMC) para 2
2   Consent: patients and doctors working together (GMC) para 5

and explore the reasons for their request. If, after discussion, the doctor still considers that the treatment would not be of overall benefit to the patient, they do not have to provide the treatment. But they should explain their reasons to the patient, and explain any other options that are available, including the option to seek a second opinion.[3]

13.2 Battery and trespass

Unless a patient has voluntarily consented to contact from a doctor, or such contact is carried out in an emergency and consent cannot reasonably be obtained[4] (or the patient lacks mental capacity), treatment involving physical contact will amount to a trespass to the person – an assault or a battery – or a criminal assault (see Section 15.6(iii) below). All adults with capacity can give voluntary and informed consent. Different rules apply in relation to children and to those unable to understand the nature of the decisions to be made (see Sections 13.4(vii) and 14 below). Once a patient is informed as to the nature of the procedure which is planned in broad terms, and consents to it, the consent is valid so far as to permit contact that would otherwise be a trespass to the person and no claim based on assault or battery can be made. The consent can be withdrawn at any time.

13.3 Civil claims – The Montgomery test

If a doctor fails to provide information about all possible serious risks, even though information is provided about the nature of the procedure in broad terms, the patient may have a remedy in a claim for damages in negligence. Until very recently the test in negligence was the *Bolam* test (see Section 15.5(i) below), that is whether the failure to warn or to provide information amounted to a failure to act in accordance with the practice accepted as proper by a responsible body of similar medical practitioners[5].

In relation to patients who are competent to give consent, claims rarely arise as to whether consent has been given. However, claims do arise as to whether the information given by the clinician in obtaining consent was appropriate.

The Supreme Court, in *Montgomery v Lanarkshire Health Board*[6], ruled that *Bolam* no longer applies to issues in relation to consenting. In that area the standard and the practice needs to take into account the importance of personal autonomy and the value of self-determination and that, in making a decision which might have a profound effect on her health and well-being, a patient was entitled to information and advice about possible alternative and variant treatments. The test is now therefore that:

---

3 Consent: patients and doctors working together (GMC) para 5

4 And there is no convincing reason to believe that consent would have been withheld

5 *Siddaway v Board of Governors of the Bethlem Royal Hospital* [1985] AC 871, *Chatterton v Gerson* [1981] QB 432

6 [2015] UKSC 11, https://www.bailii.org/uk/cases/UKSC/2015/11.pdf

A doctor is under a duty to take reasonable care to ensure that a patient is aware of any material risks involved in any recommended treatment, and of any reasonable alternative or variant treatments.

The test of materiality is whether, in the circumstances, a reasonable person in the patient's position would be likely to attach significance to the risk, or the doctor is or should reasonably be aware that the particular patient would be likely to attach significance to it[7].

A medical practitioner is therefore under a duty to warn a patient in general terms of possible material or significant risks involved in any proposed course of treatment, the materiality or significance being viewed from the viewpoint of a reasonable person in the patient's position, or in the light of anything known or which should have been known about the particular patient's circumstances. The General Medical Council Guidance *Consent: Patients and Doctors making Decisions Together*[8] is consistent with *Montgomery* and provides much further useful and relevant guidance in taking reasonable care in obtaining consent.

Treatment performed without such information is not unlawful (and therefore is not a trespass to the person) where the nature of the procedure in broad terms is explained[9]. It will however give rise to a potential claim in damages for negligence should an adverse consequence result and could form the basis for professional disciplinary proceedings.

It follows that:

If there is a significant risk[10] which would affect the judgement of a reasonable patient, then in the normal course it is the responsibility of a doctor to inform the patient of that significant risk, if the information is needed so that the patient can determine for him or herself as to what course he or she would adopt[11].

> ## A PATIENT MUST BE WARNED OF ALL SIGNIFICANT RISKS FROM PROPOSED TREATMENT

There are two situations in which a claim for negligence can be brought on the basis of a failure to obtain proper consent.

1. Where a patient is not informed of such a material risk when being consented for an operation and in the course of the operation that risk

---

7   *Montgomery* (see above) para 87

8   http://www.gmc-uk.org/static/documents/content/Consent_-_English_0914.pdf

9   See *Chatterton v Gerson* (above)

10   In court judgments relating to consent, the words 'serious' and 'significant' have both been used to describe the risks that need to be acknowledged.

11   *Pearce v United Bristol Healthcare NHS Trust* [1999] PIQR P53

manifests, the medical practitioner will be liable in damages where the patient can prove (on the balance of probabilities) that if properly warned, then she would not have agreed to undergo the treatment, and therefore would not have suffered the adverse consequence.

2.   Where the patient would have probably gone ahead with an operation, but once appropriately warned would not have proceeded on that occasion (even though the patient would probably have undergone the operation on a subsequent occasion), the medical practitioner will still be liable for damages if, on the balance of probabilities, on that subsequent occasion the complication of which the patient was not warned would not have occurred.[12]

13.4 Practicalities

(i)   By whom and when

It is the doctor who recommends the treatment to the patient who has the responsibility for seeking consent and therefore discussing the matter with the patient. Consent can, if necessary, be delegated to a suitably trained and qualified health professional. It must not be delegated to a junior or to some other person unfamiliar with the procedure being discussed.

> THE DOCTOR RECOMMENDING TREATMENT IS RESPONSIBLE FOR SEEKING APPROPRIATE CONSENT

The discussion should take place a little while prior to the planned procedure. Providing information as to the risks of a procedure in order to obtain consent immediately before a significant procedure is to be carried out is unlikely to be valid. The patient already prepared for theatre is unlikely to be able to take on board such advice and to make an informed and voluntary decision. Giving new information to a patient on the morning of the operation, having previously had an adequate discussion, is inappropriate. It is important that the patient genuinely feels able to consider and discuss the information being provided by the doctor.

On the other hand, consent obtained a long time previously should be reaffirmed, and account taken of any new information available or any change in the patient's condition, which may only be ascertained through a further discussion.

(ii) Forms and records

Consent is a process for informing the patient of the information that enables the patient to make a decision to undergo specific treatment. It therefore informs the

---

12   *Chester v Afshar* [2005] 1AC 134, https://www.bailii.org/uk/cases/UKHL/2004/41.pdf

patient of the risks that might occur despite competent treatment so as to enable the patient to reach an informed judgement as to whether to agree to undergo the procedure. In support of this process a consent form will generally list the known significant risks and complications of the procedure to be undertaken. However it must be understood that:

- Acknowledgment of the risks of the procedure by signing the consent form does not excuse any lack of care in the carrying out of the procedure, even where such lack of care results in the risk that has been acknowledged. Proper consent does not in any way limit the patient's right to competent treatment
- The form is no more, at best, than a record of what it is said the patient was told; it is not proof that the patient was in fact informed clearly and comprehensibly of all matters on the form. That will be a matter of the word of those present at the time – doctor and other medical staff, and patient and family or supporter.

In a recent case[13] the judge stated:

The simple fact that [the patient] signed the hospital consent form is not taken as an indication of acceptance of risk. In my view the document is of no real significance on the present facts [where there had been previous discussion]. It would have greater significance in emergency cases involving no prior contact between patient and clinician.

- Relying on 'usual practice' is an unsatisfactory way to prove that any particular information was given on a particular occasion. (See Chapter 8 'Records and making notes' above.)

It is advisable to record details of the discussion separately from the consent form in the patient's records together with any particular conversation which took place with the patient or family member or supporter.

It is good practice for details of the consenting discussion to be included in any letter sent to a patient's GP following the consultation at which consent was obtained. Where oral advice is given to a patient and subsequently in a letter a significant risk, previously discussed, is not mentioned although all other risks are, there is a risk that that omission will be taken to have potentially confused the patient into thinking that the significant risk previously mentioned is in fact of no real significance, or that the advice given in the discussion has been over-taken or superseded by the formal written advice in the letter. It should also be noted that the inconsistency that would also exist between the clinician's subse-quent account of the oral discussion and the contents of the letter might weaken the clinician's credibility as to what in fact occurred at the oral discussion, if that is in dispute (see Section 2.5 'Consistency and inconsistency' above).

---

13   *Thefaut v Johnston* [2017] EWHC 497, https://www.bailii.org/ew/cases/EWHC/QB/2017/497.html

(iii)   The discussion

The discussion should normally include information about:

- The patient's diagnosis and prognosis
- Options for treatment, including non-operative care and no treatment
- The purpose and expected benefit of the treatment
- The likelihood of success
- The clinicians involved in the treatment
- The risks inherent in the procedure, however small the possibility of their occurrence, side effects and complications. The consequences of non-operative alternatives should also be explained.
- Potential follow up treatment.

Written information should also be provided so that patients can reflect on the decision and identify routes to obtain further information should they require it[14]. If however the written information, whether in a patient information leaflet or in a letter, fails to mention significant risks which were discussed, then the subsequent written information may be taken to have superseded the oral discussion[15].

A discussion is likely to be much better informed on both sides if the patient has been provided with written information, such as a leaflet about the recommended treatment and its risks, in ample time before the discussion takes place.

Therapeutic exemption

There is an exception – described as 'rare' in *Montgomery* - about providing information in the context of a discussion for consent purposes in the limited circumstances in which the doctor considers that the provision of some information might cause the patient psychological harm to a degree which outweighs the benefits of providing information. This is termed 'the therapeutic exception'. This exception is limited and narrowly defined and should not be relied on for not informing the patient of a risk without a discussion first with experienced colleagues and the legal team.

(iv)   The risk

As we have seen, *Montgomery* referred to *'a significant risk which would affect the judgement of a reasonable patient'* as one which is considered *'material'* and which an adult person of sound mind is entitled to be given to decide which, if any, of the available forms of treatment to undergo.

There is no 'magic number' as to what kind of risk it is necessary to warn a

---

14   This list comes from the Royal College of Surgeon's Good Surgical Practice section 3.5.1 Consent

15   *Thefaut v Johnston* (see above)

patient of. What is important is its 'materiality' or 'significance' to the individual concerned. In a case in 2015[16] the judge found a risk of 1:1,000 was not material. In another, where the risk was put at between 1:500 and 1:10,000, the judge took it as a risk of between 1:500 and 1:1,000 and as one which was material (in that case the risk of paralysis)[17]. But in considering the alternatives of intervention under general anaesthetic and non-intervention it might well be considered material to refer to the risk of death.

(v)   Communication issues

Because consent requires the exchange of information between patient and doctor, the discussion must be tailored to the patient, and that will include the patient's level of knowledge about and understanding of her condition, prognosis and treatment options, and the patient's confirmation that she has understood the information given.

This process can be time-consuming, but it is essential. It is the doctor's responsibility to raise any concerns about any compromise of the ability to provide patients with adequate time and information for this process with their employing or contracting authority.

See Chapter 9 for a more general discussion about communication issues.

> CONSENTING REQUIRES EFFECTIVE
> COMMUNICATION BETWEEN THE DOCTOR AND
> THE PARTICULAR PATIENT

(vi)   The reluctant patient

If, after discussion, a patient still does not want to know in detail about her condition or the treatment, it remains necessary to give her the information needed in order for her to give her consent to a proposed investigation or treatment, such as what the investigation or treatment aims to achieve and what it will involve, and whether it is invasive; what level of pain or discomfort might be experienced, and what can be done to minimise it; anything the patient should do to prepare for the investigation or treatment; and if it involves any serious risks.

If the patient insists that she does not want even this basic information, then it is necessary to explain the potential consequences of her not having it, particularly if it might mean that her consent is not valid. The patient needs to be told that declining to have a discussion about the proposed investigation or treatment and

---

16   *A v East Kent University Hospitals Trust* [2015] EWHC 1038, https://www.bailii.org/ew/cases/EWHC/QB/2015/1038.html

17   *Thefaut v Johnston* (see above)

any potential risks of the different treatment options means that she is refusing to be involved in the normal consenting process. The fact that the patient has declined this information must be recorded and the patient must be told that she can change her mind and have more information at any time.

If a patient with mental capacity choses to refuse treatment, even if this is a potentially dangerous or fatal choice, then that is a choice a doctor must respect, and this has long been recognised in the law. It is of course important for the doctor to discuss those implications with the patient so that the patient's decision is informed, even if it is not the decision that the doctor would recommend.

(vii)   Children and young people

In this section the word 'child' will be used to cover 'child or young person'.

There is no cut-off age after which a person's own consent is required.

> *A young person's ability to make decisions depends more on their ability to understand and weigh up options, than on their age. When assessing a young person's capacity to make decisions, you should bear in mind that:*
>
> *a) a young person under 16 may have capacity to make decisions, depending on their maturity and ability to understand what is involved*
>
> *b) at 16 a young person can be presumed to have capacity to make most decisions about their treatment and care .*

It is necessary to assess whether a child is able to understand the nature, purpose and possible consequences of investigations or treatments that are being proposed and the consequences of not undergoing them. If the child can understand, retain, use and weigh the information and communicate her decision then she has the capacity to consent (see Chapter 14 'Mental capacity and mental disorder' below).

Although a child at 16 is presumed to have such capacity, it is necessary to assess the child under 16 who may still have the capacity to consent depending on her maturity and ability to understand what is involved in the decision (as well as being open to the possibility of a child of 16 or 17 lacking capacity through immaturity or the complex nature of the decision or some other factor). That capacity may relate only to relatively simple decisions, such as for risk-free treatment, or may be sufficient for more complicated decision-making. Each child must be assessed on her degree of maturity and understanding in the context of the decision to be made. Even where the child is assessed as having capacity, she should be encouraged to involve her parents in important decisions, although the decision will normally remain the decision of the child.

If the child is assessed as lacking capacity to consent, then the parent's consent should be sought. If parents are not in agreement then it may be necessary to apply to the court. If a child aged 16 or 17 is assessed as not having capacity (despite the presumption in favour of capacity) then parents can provide the necessary consent to investigations or treatment in the child's best interest, and (in England and Wales only) treatment can be provided in the child's best interests without parental consent, although the parental views may be important in assessing what is in the child's best interests.

The guiding principle is that a doctor should act in a child or young person's best interests at all times. However, defining what is in that child's best interests may not be straightforward. While there may be an objective clinical view on best interests, the views of the child and of her parents or others close to her must also be taken into account.

A new set of communication issues, beyond those when dealing with an adult, arise when discussing issues with a child but the child should still be informed, in appropriate terms, of the relevant information about the treatment and treatment options. In some circumstances the involvement of a person with particular expertise in such communication will be appropriate.

If a child refuses treatment, particular care is needed. Where the healthcare professional considers that treatment which is refused by a child with capacity is in the child's best interests, then legal advice should be sought.

Further reading

Consent: Patients and doctors making decisions together (GMC)[18]

Consent tool kit (BMA)[19]

Good Surgical Practice (Royal College of Surgeons) section 3.5.1 Consent[20]

Consent: supported decision-making (Royal College of Surgeons)[21]

0-18 years: guidance for all doctors (GMC)[22]

The dento-legal guide to consent (DDU)[23]

---

18   http://www.gmc-uk.org/guidance/ethical_guidance/consent_guidance_index.asp

19   https://www.bma.org.uk/advice/employment/ethics/consent

20   https://www.rcseng.ac.uk/standards-and-research/gsp/domain-3/3-5-1-consent/

21   https://www.rcseng.ac.uk/-/media/files/rcs/library-and-publications/non-journal-publications/consent_2016_combined-p2.pdf

22   https://www.gmc-uk.org/static/documents/content/0_18_years.pdf

23   https://www.theddu.com/guidance-and-advice/guides/consent

14

Mental capacity and mental disorder

Chapter outline

This Chapter will look at the issues that arise when treating patients who lack mental capacity and those suffering from mental disorders. The legal test for capacity is looked at and considered in practice, along with the meaning of 'best interests'. Dementia and long-term incapacities raise similar issues and are also considered.

Questions may arise about the capacity of a patient who needs treatment, but does not wish to remain for such treatment, and this Chapter will look at the different circumstances in which different people are empowered to detain the patient.

14.1 The statutory framework (mental capacity)

For a person to make a valid decision or to give consent to treatment, she must have mental capacity, that is the ability to make a decision for herself. The

Mental Capacity Act 2005[1] sets out the test that has to be addressed in answering the question of whether someone has such mental capacity. This applies to persons aged 16 or over.

The Act sets out the principles to be applied as follows:

1. The principles

(1) The following principles apply for the purposes of this Act.

(2) A person must be assumed to have capacity unless it is established that he lacks capacity.

(3) A person is not to be treated as unable to make a decision unless all practicable steps to help him to do so have been taken without success.

(4) A person is not to be treated as unable to make a decision merely because he makes an unwise decision.

The statutory presumption at Section 1(2) means that it is for the person seeking to establish lack of capacity to prove that lack of capacity. (Section 2(4) below provides that proof must be on the balance of probabilities.) It follows from Section 1(3) that it is necessary to consider what steps could be taken to assist the patient to make a decision – for example, the support of a parent or spouse or someone else familiar with the patient or with the patient's condition. Perhaps more difficult is the provision at Section 1(4) that a person is entitled to make an unwise decision without being regarded as lacking capacity so that a patient is entitled to refuse treatment which the clinician regards as advisable without necessarily being regarded as lacking capacity. The test is also decision specific, so that a person may have capacity for the purpose of making some decisions but not for others.

> A PERSON IS PRESUMED TO HAVE CAPACITY UNLESS
> IT IS PROVED THEY DO NOT

Section 2 is concerned with the characteristics of the person under consideration.

2. People who lack capacity

(1) For the purposes of this Act, a person lacks capacity in relation to a matter if at the material time he is unable to make a decision for himself in relation to the matter because of an impairment of, or a disturbance in the functioning of, the mind or brain.

(2) It does not matter whether the impairment or disturbance is permanent

---

1   https://www.legislation.gov.uk/ukpga/2005/9/contents

or temporary.

(3) A lack of capacity cannot be established merely by reference to—

    (a) a person's age or appearance, or

    (b) a condition of his, or an aspect of his behaviour, which might lead others to make unjustified assumptions about his capacity.

(4) In proceedings under this Act or any other enactment, any question whether a person lacks capacity within the meaning of this Act must be decided on the balance of probabilities.

Capacity is to be considered at the time that a decision is to be made. The inability to make a decision must be caused by an impairment or disturbance of the mind or brain, whether permanent or temporary (Section 2(1) and 2(2)). The test is applied regardless of the person's age, appearance, behaviour etc (Section 2(3)). For the avoidance of doubt, Section 2(4) states that questions about capacity must be decided on the balance of probabilities.

CAPACITY IS DECISION SPECIFIC

Further important guidance as to how the inability to make decisions must be assessed is set out in Section 3.

3. Inability to make decisions

(1) For the purposes of section 2, a person is unable to make a decision for himself if he is unable—

    (a) to understand the information relevant to the decision,

    (b) to retain that information,

    (c) to use or weigh that information as part of the process of making the decision, or

    (d) to communicate his decision (whether by talking, using sign language or any other means).

(2) A person is not to be regarded as unable to understand the information relevant to a decision if he is able to understand an explanation of it given to him in a way that is appropriate to his circumstances (using simple language, visual aids or any other means).

(3) The fact that a person is able to retain the information relevant to a decision for a short period only does not prevent him from being regarded as able

to make the decision.

(4) The information relevant to a decision includes information about the reasonably foreseeable consequences of—

(a) deciding one way or another, or

(b) failing to make the decision.

Section 3(1) sets out the 4-part test which is at the heart of the question of capacity and which is to be applied in assessing the inability to make decisions. Lack of capacity only arises if the person cannot understand the information relevant to the decision, cannot retain that information and cannot use or weigh that information as part of the decision-making process and cannot communicate the decision. The relevant information will include the information as to the reasonably foreseeable consequences of either deciding an issue one way or the other or failing to make a decision (Section 3(4)). Someone who cannot retain information may nonetheless have capacity if the information is retained for long enough in order to make a decision.

14.2 The test in practice

When addressing the issue of whether a person has mental capacity in relation to an identified decision to be taken it is necessary to follow through a series of questions, applying the standard of proof (on the balance of probabilities) before reaching a conclusion as to whether or not the presumption of capacity is rebutted.

1. Does the person have an impairment of the mind or brain, or is there some sort of disturbance affecting the way their mind or brain works, whether the impairment or disturbance is temporary or permanent? (the 'diagnostic threshold')

2. If so, does that impairment or disturbance mean that the person is unable to make the decision in question at the time it needs to be made? (the 'functional' test)

Then it is necessary to go on to assess the ability to make a decision by answering the following questions:

1. Does the person have a general understanding of what decision they need to make and why they need to make it?

2. Does the person have a general understanding of the likely consequences of making, or not making, this decision?

3. Is the person able to understand, retain, use and weigh up the information relevant to this decision?

4.   Can the person communicate his or her decision (by talking, using sign language or any other means)? Would the services of a professional (such as a speech and language therapist) be helpful?

TESTING FOR CAPACITY
- UNDERSTAND THE DECISION?
- UNDERSTAND THE CONSEQUENCES?
- USE THE INFORMATION?
- COMMUNICATE THE DECISION?

By working through this series of questions and providing the answers, it should be possible to provide the required conclusion as to whether the person is proved, on the balance of probabilities, to lack capacity in relation to the decision to be made.

In a borderline case it may be that the patient is considered to retain capacity if, but only if, assisted and supported by family or professional helpers. In such a case the finding of capacity is of course dependent on the patient receiving such support.

As we have seen above, Section 1(3) requires that a person is not to be treated as unable to make a decision unless all practicable steps to help her to do so have been taken without success.

The Mental Capacity Act 2005 Code of Practice (issued by the Lord Chancellor on 23 April 2007) at paragraph 3 states:

> Before deciding that someone lacks capacity to make a particular decision, it is important to take all practical and appropriate steps to enable them to make that decision themselves (statutory principle 2). In addition, as section 3(2) of the Act underlines, these steps (such as helping individuals to communicate) must be taken in a way which reflects the person's individual circumstances and meets their particular needs. This chapter provides practical guidance on how to support people to make decisions for themselves, or play as big a role as possible in decision-making.

The decision must then be recorded in the medical notes (see Chapter 8 'Records and making notes' above). That will require the following to be covered:

- The specific decision for which capacity is assessed
- The manner in which capacity is assessed
- The reasons for concluding that the patient lacks capacity
- The outcome and consequences of the decision (the treatment plan).

The decision as to lack of capacity is made on the balance of probabilities: 'I believe that on the balance of probabilities X lacks capacity to make the decision to ….…..[nature of decision] because ….….. [reasons relied upon]'. The record should indicate that the numbered questions posed at the beginning of this section have been addressed.

These issues are likely to arise most urgently in emergency medicine. The RCEM guidance *The Mental Capacity Act in Emergency Medicine Practice* (RCEM) February 2017[2] provides useful guidance and examples of common situations.

14.3 Best interests

If a patient lacks capacity, then a decision must be made on her behalf and in her 'best interests'. In making such a decision it is necessary to:

1. encourage the person to take part as far as possible;

2. identify what the person would have taken into account if they were making the decision;

3. find out the person's prior views, wishes and beliefs (for example any living will or other written statement of wishes on treatment);

4. consult others, where appropriate, about the person's views, wishes and beliefs;

5. make an objective assessment of what would be in their 'best interests'.

In difficult or urgent cases an emergency application can be made to the Court of Protection[3].

14.4 Dementia and long-term incapacity

Caring for people with dementia or other long-term lack of mental capacity may involve reducing their independence or restricting their free-will in some way. If they are receiving care in a hospital or care home, their routine will be decided for them, and they may not be allowed to leave. If the person has not freely chosen these things, it will take away some of their freedom. This may amount to a 'deprivation of liberty'.

Under the Mental Capacity Act 2005 any care that restricts a person's liberty must be appropriate and in their best interests. Any hospital or care home which intends to deprive such a person of their liberty must obtain permission to do so. The first step is a DoLS assessment ('Deprivation of Liberty Safeguards') which is requested from the local authority. A personal representative (often a family member) will be appointed and the assessment will be regularly reviewed.

---

2   https://www.rcem.ac.uk//docs/College Guidelines/A brief guide to Section 136 for Emergency Departments - Dec 2017.pdf

3   https://www.gov.uk/emergency-court-of-protection

It is important to bear in mind that capacity (or incapacity) may be intermittent and, as we have discussed above, that it is decision specific.

14.5 Detaining a person for emergency treatment

(i) The outpatient attending A&E

If a patient who has attended for emergency treatment decides to leave the emergency department because she is not able to understand that she is unwell and unable to weigh the consequences of not being assessed and treated for her condition, then the lack of capacity is due to her mental health. The patient does not have the capacity to decide to leave and she can be stopped from leaving using the Mental Capacity Act, but will need a Mental Health Act (MHA) assessment if she is to be detained for any length of time, which would then determine whether there should be further detention under Sections 2, 3 or 4 of the MHA. The means used to detain the patient must be proportionate to the situation.

(ii) The inpatient

If the patient of concern was on a ward as an inpatient when trying to leave, then she could be detained using Section 5(2) of the MHA. The section provides that, in the case of any inpatient in hospital, if it appears to the registered medical practitioner or approved clinician in charge of the treatment of the patient that an application ought to be made under Sections 2, 3 or 4 of the MHA for the admission of the patient to hospital, he may furnish to the managers a report in writing to that effect; and in any such case the patient may be detained in the hospital for a period of 72 hours from the time when the report is so furnished. For convenience, the registered medical practitioner or approved clinician in charge of the treatment of a patient in a hospital may nominate one (but not more than one) person to act for him under subsection (2) above in his absence.

(iii) Section 136 detention by police

If a person found in a place other than their home (or the garden or buildings associated with it) appears to a police officer to be suffering from mental disorder and to be in immediate need of care or control, the police officer may, if he thinks it necessary to do so in the interests of that person or for the protection of other persons—

(a) remove the person to a place of safety, usually a hospital but sometimes in exceptional circumstances (and in the case of an adult only) a police station, or

(b) if the person is already at a place of safety, keep the person at that place or remove the person to another place of safety,

under Section 136 of the Mental Health Act 2005. Therefore a police officer can under this section detain a person who is in the street, in a public place or in a hospital.

Before deciding to remove a person to, or to keep a person at, a place of safety under Section 136, the police officer must, if it is practicable to do so, consult—

(a) a registered medical practitioner,

(b) a registered nurse, or

(c) an approved mental health professional.

On arrival at hospital under Section 136 the nurse in charge and a senior clinician should review the patient with the police and ambulance crew to assess her medical needs and review her risks to self and others. Referral for a MHA assessment should be made as soon as possible (on arrival at hospital or as soon as she is medically fit for assessment although it may be possible for physical and mental health assessments to be carried out in parallel).

The person may be detained in hospital for a period not exceeding 24 hours for the purpose of enabling her to be examined by a registered medical practitioner and to be interviewed by an approved mental health professional and of making any necessary arrangements for her treatment or care. The patient can then be assessed for possible admission under Sections 2, 3 or 4 of the MHA.

It is important to note that:

1. the patient should be kept informed of her rights and kept updated of the plan for her care and assessment;

2. police are responsible for the safety of the patient under s 136 and should the police be allowed to leave, the emergency department takes on this responsibility and should be confident that it has the staff and resources to deal with the risk of the patient absconding. While if the patient is in a coma little risk is likely to arise in this situation, otherwise very careful consideration should be given before agreeing to the police leaving;

3. the police may search the patient if they have reasonable grounds to suspect a risk of self-harm or risk of harm to others.

(iv)   Inpatient receiving mental health treatment

In the case of a person already receiving treatment for mental disorder as an inpatient in hospital, if it appears to a nurse of the prescribed class (specially qualified and trained to work with mental health problems or learning disabilities)—

(a) that the patient is suffering from mental disorder to such a degree that it is necessary for his health or safety or for the protection of others for him to be immediately restrained from leaving the hospital; and

(b) that it is not practicable to secure the immediate attendance of a practitioner or clinician for the purpose of furnishing a report under subsection 5(2) to justify further detention,

under Section 5(4) of the MHA the nurse may record that fact in writing (and supply the record to the hospital managers as soon as possible after it is made); and in that event the patient may be detained in the hospital for a period of six hours from the time when that fact is so recorded or until the earlier arrival at the place where the patient is detained of a practitioner or clinician having power to furnish a report under that subsection.

Further reading

Mental Capacity Act 2005[4]

Mental Capacity Act Code of Practice[5]

Making decisions: a guide for people who work in health and social care[6]

Online toolkit – Assessing Mental Capacity (BMA)[7]

Deprivation of Liberty Safeguards (DoLS) (for people with dementia) (Alzheimer's Society)[8]

Mental Health Act 2005[9]

A brief guide to Section 136 for Emergency Departments (RCEM) December 2017[10]

The Mental Capacity Act in Emergency Medicine Practice (RCEM) February 2017[11]

---

4   https://www.legislation.gov.uk/ukpga/2005/9/contents

5   https://www.gov.uk/government/uploads/system/uploads/attachment_data/file/497253/
     Mental-capacity-act-code-of-practice.pdf

6   https://www.gov.uk/government/uploads/system/uploads/attachment_data/file/348440/
     OPG603-Health-care-workers-MCA-decisions.pdf

7   http://synthetix-ec2.com/clients/bma_v3/

8   https://www.alzheimers.org.uk/download/downloads/id/2671/deprivation_of_liberty_safe-
     guards_dols.pdf

9   http://www.legislation.gov.uk/ukpga/1983/20/contents

10   https://www.rcem.ac.uk//docs/College Guidelines/A brief guide to Section 136 for Emer-
     gency Departments - Dec 2017.pdf

11   https://www.rcem.ac.uk/docs/RCEM Guidance/RCEM Mental Capacity Act in EM
     Practice - Feb 2017.pdf

15

When things go wrong

Chapter outline

With the best will in the world, and with the greatest care and skill, things will sometimes go wrong when treating a patient. This may be through no fault at all although that may not be how it is seen by the patient or the patient's relatives. It may be the result of inappropriate action or inaction on the part of the clinician or of someone else in the team or within the organisation or because of a 'system' failure or because of a combination of these factors. Whatever the cause, this is a stressful part of a clinician's life, but that stress can be reduced by better understanding the various processes surrounding such events.

This Chapter begins with consideration of the duty of candour and whistleblowing, and goes on to explain the different kinds of investigations that can take place following an adverse event, from serious incident investigations, claims for damages in negligence, potential criminal proceedings to regulatory proceedings (fitness to practise) and the role of inquests. Finally, the Chapter looks at disciplinary proceedings, CQC inspections and the need for insurance and the places to look for support.

15.1 Introduction

A recent estimate suggested that there are 12,000 avoidable hospital deaths every year, and more than 24,000 serious incidents are reported to NHS England annually (the total annual number of reports to NHS England including low-harm and no-harm incidents is 1.4 million)[1].

It is inevitable in clinical practice that sometimes 'things go wrong'. That events have not turned out as was hoped does not mean that any criticism can be levelled at any individual or group of individuals. There may be an opportunity for reflective learning or to improve practices or to reflect on the vagaries of life.

When things do go wrong in clinical practice, however, it may give rise to a number of potential proceedings, inquiries and claims as well as emotional and personal reactions, which are summarised in the following table. They are not mutually exclusive, so one, two or more may follow from an untoward event.

Action	Purpose/outcome
Serious incident investigation	To identify any weaknesses in systems and to make recommendations for the future
Civil claim	To establish whether there has been negligence and if so to recover damages for compensation

---

1   https://publications.parliament.uk/pa/jt201719/jtselect/jthssib/1064/106403.htm

Criminal prosecution	To establish whether a crime was committed and if so to obtain a conviction resulting in imprisonment or fine
Fitness to practise/GMC investigation	To establish whether a professional is fit to practise and to sanction an individual through warnings, restrictions on practice, suspension or erasure
Coroner's inquest	To determine the circumstances of a patient's death
Disciplinary proceedings	To establish if any employment terms have been breached and to impose performance management, warnings or dismissal
Care Quality Commission inspection	To establish if standards have been breached and to impose a fine or other corrective action on the organisation.

In the following sections we will consider each of these possible courses of action but we will start with discussion of the duty of candour, which means that, whether or not proceedings or investigations may follow, a practitioner must be open with a patient and with colleagues and the healthcare provider organisation when things go wrong. We will also consider public interest disclosure ('whistle-blowing') which may arise where things are seen to be going wrong or having the potential to go wrong.

Moves are afoot to establish a 'safe space' for NHS staff including clinicians to be open about what happened when a patient dies or is harmed unnecessarily. At the time of writing the Health Service Safety Investigations Bill is working its way through parliament. The new body would be prohibited from disclosing information given to it, but would use the information to make recommendations, so as to overcome the perceived fear of speaking out.

15.2 Duty of candour

You must be open and honest with patients if things go wrong. If a patient under your care has suffered harm or distress, you should:

(a) put matters right (if that is possible)

(b) offer an apology

(c) explain fully and promptly what has happened and the likely short-term and long-term effects[2].

---

2   Good Medical Practice (GMC) para 55

Every healthcare professional has a duty to be honest with patients when things go wrong with treatment or care and this causes or has the potential to cause harm or distress. In addition, every healthcare professional must also be open and honest with colleagues, employers and relevant organisations, and with their regulators. They must also support and encourage each other to be open and honest.

The heart of the requirement, applicable equally to doctors, nurses and midwives, is to:

- speak to a patient, or those close to them, as soon as possible after they realise something has gone wrong with their care
- apologise to the patient, explaining what happened, what can be done if they have suffered harm and what will be done to prevent someone else being harmed in the future
- report errors at an early stage so that lessons can be learned quickly, and patients are protected from harm in the future.

The requirement is also to be open with patients, colleagues and employers. When working in a team the requirement is to make sure that someone in the team, usually the lead or accountable clinician, has taken on that responsibility, and to support them as necessary.

Candour starts with openness and honesty before treatment or care is started. A patient should be spoken to as soon as it is realised that something has gone wrong with her care, even if treatment or investigations are continuing, and there should be a friend or relative (or some other suitable present) present to support the patient. In the case of death, a relative should be spoken to and should be supported. The information provided should be all that the healthcare professional knows about what went wrong and why and the likely consequences. An apology should be given.

Information should not be forced on a patient who does not want it, but in that case it is necessary to try to find out why the patient does not want to know, to record the fact, and to tell the patient that she can change her mind and have more information at any time.

> THE DUTY OF CANDOUR REQUIRES OPENNESS
> AND HONESTY WITH A PATIENT WHEN THINGS GO
> WRONG

A patient should be told:

- what happened
- what can be done to deal with any harm caused
- what will be done to prevent someone else being harmed.

An apology is not the same as an admission of legal liability. Apart from being the right thing to do, it is likely to be regarded in any future investigation as evidence of insight on the part of the healthcare professional.

To be an effective apology:

- information must be given in a way that the patient can understand
- it should be given at a time when the patient is best able to understand and retain the information
- it should be given in a considerate way which respects the patient's right to privacy and dignity
- it should be given in a personalised way – 'I am sorry ….' – even though that does not mean that the person apologising is necessarily taking personal responsibility for the error
- the patient must be given information as to who to contact in the healthcare team and in support services to provide further information and support.

The apology should be recorded in the patient's clinical record. Consideration should be given to providing a subsequent written apology.

The duty of candour is also intended to encourage a learning culture through the reporting of errors and to protect patients from harm in the future. A healthcare organisation's system for reporting adverse incidents is therefore closely related to this duty and the organisation should support the practitioner in reporting adverse incidents and near misses as a matter of routine.

A healthcare organisation, but not an individual healthcare professional, has a statutory duty of candour under Regulation 20 of the Health and Social Care Act 2008 (Regulated Activities) Regulations 2014 and can be prosecuted for breaches of the Regulation.

15.3 Public interest disclosure ('whistleblowing')

You must promote and encourage a culture that allows all staff to raise concerns openly and safely[3].

You must take prompt action if you think that patient safety, dignity or comfort is or may be seriously compromised.

a If a patient is not receiving basic care to meet their needs, you must immediately tell someone who is in a position to act straight away.

b If patients are at risk because of inadequate premises, equipment or other resources, policies or systems, you should put the matter right if that is possible. You must raise your concern in line with our guidance and your work-

---

3   Good Medical Practice (GMC) para 24

place policy. You should also make a record of the steps you have taken.

c If you have concerns that a colleague may not be fit to practise and may be putting patients at risk, you must ask for advice from a colleague, your defence body or us. If you are still concerned you must report this, in line with our guidance and your workplace policy, and make a record of the steps you have taken[4].

(i) Legal framework

Whistleblowing is potentially an emotive expression. This section is concerned with healthcare professionals raising concerns where there is a public interest in that happening.

There is a duty on doctors to act to protect patients. There is legal protection against victimisation or dismissal in reporting matters of concern in fulfilling this duty. Such reports, even if mistaken, are protected if made on the basis of reasonable belief and through appropriate channels.

The Public Interest Disclosure Act 2013, by amending the Employment Rights Act 1996, protects workers from detrimental treatment or victimisation from their employer if, in the public interest, they raise concerns ('blow the whistle on wrongdoing'). Within the NHS this applies to self-employed professionals[5] as well as employees. If an employee is dismissed because she has made what is termed a 'protected disclosure' then the dismissal is treated as unfair, with the usual remedies available, but in addition employees may make a complaint to an employment tribunal if, short of dismissal, they suffer any detriment as a result of making a protected disclosure.

In England doctors in training are similarly protected with regard to their relationship with Health Education England (HEE) as a result of a legally binding agreement between HEE, the BMA, the BDA and employers[6].

A protected disclosure means a disclosure made to the employer that the person making it reasonably believes tends to show that there is happening now, took place in the past or is likely to happen in the future:

- a criminal offence
- the breach of a legal obligation
- a miscarriage of justice
- a danger to the health and safety of any individual

---

4   Good Medical Practice (GMC) para 25

5   Those self-employed professionals providing general medical services, general dental services, general ophthalmic services or pharmaceutical services in accordance with arrangements under the HNS Act 1977 – see PIDA Part IVA Section 43K

6   A similar arrangement is in place in Scotland, but at the time of writing not yet in Wales or Northern Ireland – see https://www.bma.org.uk/advice/employment/contracts/junior-doctor-contract/whistleblowing

- damage to the environment
- deliberate concealment of information tending to show any of the above five matters.

The second and fourth bullet points are likely to be most relevant in the context of 'things going wrong' in a healthcare setting, but it is important to note their wording. For example, a staff shortage or equipment shortage may not necessarily amount to either a breach of a legal obligation or a danger to the health and safety of a patient, even if it is undesirable.

There are also circumstances in which a disclosure will be a 'protected' disclosure if made to some person other than an employer provided the person making it:

- makes the disclosure in good faith
- reasonably believes that the information disclosed and any allegation contained in it are substantially true
- does not make the disclosure for purposes of personal gain
- and, for example, a disclosure of substantially the same information has previously been made to the employer and it is reasonable in all the circumstances to make the disclosure.

The concern raised should be one which affects the public, rather than being related to matters impacting personally on the complainant. Something which might be a danger to the health and safety of patients could be said to affect the public. In contrast matters impacting personally on the complainant may be appropriate for raising through the employer's normal grievance procedure.

NHS England, in *Voicing your concerns for Staff (whistleblowing policy)*[7], sets out the support that that organisation says it has for staff who raise concerns in the public interest and makes clear that requests for confidentiality and anonymity will be respected.

(ii)   Practicalities

All employers should have a formal policy for raising concerns. A healthcare professional should therefore raise any concern in accordance with local policy, which should allow issues to be addressed and remedied. Normally this will provide for raising them through the line manager, the consultant in charge of the team, the clinical or medical director or a practice partner, depending on the circumstances. There should be a designated person as an alternative in the event that complaints are about management. A doctor in training may raise concerns with a named person in the deanery, as for example the postgraduate dean or director of postgraduate general practice education.

If, because the responsible person or body locally is believed to be part of the

---

7   https://www.england.nhs.uk/wp-content/uploads/2016/09/voicing-concerns-staff-policy.pdf

problem, there are difficulties raising the issue or if having raised the concern through local channels it is felt that the responsible person or body has not taken adequate action or if there is an immediate serious risk to patients, and a regulator or other external body has responsibility to act or intervene, then the regulatory body with authority to investigate the issue should be contacted, such as the GMC, GDC, NMC or HEE.

If all steps have been taken to attempt to deal with a concern by raising it within the organisation at which the complainant works or has a contract, or with the appropriate external body, and there is good reason to believe that patients are still at risk of harm, and it will not breach patient confidentiality, then it may be appropriate to make the concerns public. However before doing so it is highly advisable to seek advice, for example from the complainant's regulatory body or medical defence organisation.

Trainees and students in healthcare who think patient safety and quality of care are at risk should report any issues with their employer, that is at the trust where they are employed. However, Health Education England is one of the prescribed organisations to which employees can report concerns in circumstances where they are unable to do so to their employer.

The general route for raising concerns is, in the first instance, to the identified line manager or alternatively the designated person. If concerns are not addressed properly at that level, then the concerns should be raised to the medical director. If they are still not addressed satisfactorily, then the issues can be escalated to the chief executive (informing the medical director that that is what is being done).

Concerns raised should be investigated promptly and confidentially by the employer and the outcome of the investigation should be reported back to the complainant in writing.

Further advice on issues arising in relation to whistleblowing can be obtained from a number of sources including the medical defence organisations and the BMA, which all offer helplines .

(iii)   Record keeping

The basis for the raising of the concern must be recorded. It is important to make and keep records and notes containing as much detail as possible, and they should be made as close in time to the events recorded as possible. Subsequent material events should also be recorded, as also all steps taken to raise the concern.

The emphasis should be on identifying facts, and avoiding hearsay (see Section 3.1(ii)), rumour and emotion, and communicating the matters of concern and the evidence in relation to it in a professional manner.

15.4 Serious incident investigation

A voluntary reporting system, the National Reporting and Learning System (NRLS), exists for any 'Patient Safety Incidents', that is any unintended or unexpected incidents that could have led, or did lead, to harm for one or more NHS patients. This is integrated with other reporting systems so that it captures all patient safety incidents reported to local risk management systems such as Datix or Ulyses. When reporting patient safety incidents to the NRLS the actual (not potential) level of harm caused must be reported. The Strategic Executive Information System (STEIS) captures all Serious Incidents as defined in the Serious Incident Framework (see below). An incident resulting in no or low harm may still be a Serious Incident (see below); it is not the outcome which is determinative.

It is mandatory for NHS trusts in England to report all serious patient safety incidents to the Care Quality Commission, and this must be done within 2 working days of the incident. This is also done through NRLS. These reports to NRLS are analysed to identify common hazards and to recommend actions to mitigate risks and improve the safety of patient care.

If a serious adverse event occurs, then it is likely that the healthcare provider organisation will conduct an investigation following the framework laid down by the NHS. The Serious Incident Framework[8] applies to all services providing NHS funded care, including independent providers where NHS funded services are delivered.

The Framework describes 'Serious Incidents' as including acts or omissions in care that result in –

- unexpected or avoidable death
- unexpected or avoidable injury resulting in serious harm - including those where the injury required treatment to prevent death or serious harm
- abuse
- Never Events, that is serious incidents that are entirely preventable because guidance or safety recommendations providing strong systemic protective barriers are available and should have been implemented[9]
- incidents that prevent (or threaten to prevent) an organisation's ability to continue to deliver an acceptable quality of healthcare services
- incidents that cause widespread public concern resulting in a loss of confidence in healthcare services.

A 'near miss' may be classed as a Serious Incident depending on the potential severity of harm should a similar incident occur again.

Investigations under the Framework are conducted, not to hold any individual

---

8   https://improvement.nhs.uk/uploads/documents/serious-incidnt-framwrk.pdf

9   https://improvement.nhs.uk/uploads/documents/never-evnts-pol-framwrk.pdf

or organisation to account, but to ensure that Serious Incidents are identified correctly, investigated thoroughly and, most importantly, learned from to prevent the likelihood of similar incidents happening again. However, they can link in with criminal, disciplinary and regulatory processes. This means that the evidence collected and the results of the investigation will be considered by interested parties to help decide whether to take criminal or civil proceedings or to commence disciplinary or regulatory proceedings. Therefore, it is important if contributing to any such investigation to ensure that the evidence provided, whether oral or in a witness statement or other documentary form, is complete and clear, and consistent (see Section 2.5 'Consistency and inconsistency' above). The contents of the contemporaneous medical notes and records will be an important part of the investigation and therefore it is important that they are complete and accurate (see Chapter 8 'Records and making notes' above).

Once a Serious Incident is declared it will be conducted in accordance with the system-based Root Cause Analysis. In the case of less complex incidents, concise investigations will be carried out by a small group of individuals at a local level. More complex incidents will require a more *comprehensive investigation* which will be managed by a multidisciplinary team involving experts and/or specialist investigators. In cases where the integrity of the internal investigation is likely to be challenged or where it may be difficult to conduct an internal investigation objectively because of the size of the organisation, an *independent investigation* will be conducted. Concise and comprehensive investigations should be completed within 60 days and independent investigations within 6 months.

During the information gathering stage relevant people may be interviewed and clinical notes and records will be reviewed. It may be appropriate, or required, that an individual provides a statement of their involvement. The guidance on the writing of witness statements in Chapter 6 above should be referred to in providing such a statement.

Following analysis, recommendations should be developed to prevent another safety incident, and it may be that there are good processes and outcomes illustrated by the process.

Those involved should have the opportunity to access professional advice from their relevant professional body, as well as from staff counselling services and occupational health services.

It is again emphasised that the underlying principle is that a Serious Incident demonstrates weaknesses in a system that need to be addressed to prevent future incidents leading to avoidable death or serious harm to patients or staff or future significant reputational damage to the organisations involved. It is not therefore about finding out what person is to blame, although that may be an incidental outcome.

The investigation is separate from any potential legal or professional proceedings, although the investigation may feed into the decision to bring other proceedings.

15.5 Civil claim for damages in negligence

Suffering an injury does not provide an automatic right to recover compensation. Damages will only be awarded to compensate for provable loss caused by a breach of a duty of care – a legally imposed duty of care or a statutory duty – owed to the claimant by the defendant. To succeed in a claim for damages for personal injury, it is necessary for the claimant to prove:

(i)   that the defendant is in breach of a duty owed to the claimant;

(ii) that injury, loss or damage has been caused to the claimant (sufficient to form the basis of a claim in law) as a result of the breach of duty; and

(iii) the nature and extent of the injury, loss or damage sustained.

Negligence is such a breach of duty and is generally defined as:-

> ...the omission to do something which a reasonable man, guided upon those considerations which ordinarily regulate the conduct of human affairs, would do, or doing something which a prudent and reasonable man would not do[10].

That is the test applied, for example, if when driving, cycling, walking or riding a horse a person is involved in an accident in order to establish whether that person, or any other person involved, is negligent and so in breach of duty and therefore liable to pay compensation for damage caused.

However in circumstances where a person has a particular skill – such as a doctor – the test is refined. In clinical matters there are 2 different tests which are applied in ascertaining whether or not there has been a breach of duty, depending on whether the issue is one of diagnosis or treatment, or of informing a patient of risks and obtaining consent for treatment.

(i)   Bolam

In treatment and diagnosis the test is the *Bolam* test, that is that:

> A doctor is not guilty of negligence if he has acted in accordance with a practice accepted as proper by a responsible body of medical men skilled in that particular art... Putting it the other way round, a doctor is not negligent, if he is acting in accordance with such a practice, merely because there is a body of opinion that takes a contrary view[11].

Therefore, to establish whether a person with any expertise has been negligent, it is necessary to measure her actions against the standard reasonably to be expected of a reasonably competent practitioner, not against the very best or even

---

10   *Blyth v Birmingham Waterworks Co* (1856) 11 Ex Ch 781 at 784

11   *Bolam v Friern Hospital Management Committee* [1957] 2 All ER 118.

the very worst practitioner, in that field. It follows that the standard of care to be
expected of a reasonably competent practitioner is effectively set by practitioners
in that same field, not by the lawyers or by the court. Negligence will only be
established in the light of the expert opinion of a practitioner in that same field
on the actions (or inaction) of a fellow practitioner. If no practitioner will say that
the standard fell below that reasonably to be expected from a reasonably compe-
tent practitioner, it is unlikely that liability can be established.

The clearest way to express that the standard required of the *Bolam* test has not
been met is to state that *'no reasonably competent clinician would have acted (or
would have failed to act) in this manner'.*

Bolam is also authority for the principle that:-

> A judge's 'preference' for one body of distinguished professional opinion to
> another also professionally distinguished is not sufficient to establish negli-
> gence in a practitioner whose actions have received the seal of approval of
> those whose opinions, truthfully expressed, honestly held, were not preferred...
> For in the realm of diagnosis and treatment negligence is not established by
> preferring one respectable body of professional opinion to another. Failure to
> exercise the ordinary skill of a doctor (in the appropriate speciality, if he be a
> specialist) is necessary[12].

However an expert must be able to show that the practice relied on has a logical
basis and:-

> In particular in cases involving, as they so often do, the weighing of risks
> against benefits, the judge before accepting a body of opinion as being respon-
> sible, reasonable or respectable, will need to be satisfied that, in forming their
> views, the experts have directed their minds to the question of comparative
> risks and benefits and have reached a defensible conclusion on the matter[13].

This modification of the *Bolam* test is referred to by the case name in which it
was first stated, *Bolitho*.

(ii)   Montgomery

Until the Supreme Court decision in 2015 in the case of *Montgomery v Lanark-
shire Health Board*[14] the principle in *Bolam* applied also to the consenting of
patients. However that case ruled that *Bolam* was no longer applicable to the
process of providing information to a patient about the risks of a procedure in
order to obtain consent to treatment. Instead, as set out in *Montgomery*:-

12   *Maynard v West Midlands Regional Health Authority* [1984] 1 WLR 634

13   *Bolitho v City and Hackney Health Authority* [1997] 3 WLR 1151 at 1158, https://www.bailii.
org/uk/cases/UKHL/1997/46.html

14   [2015] UKSC 11, https://www.bailii.org/uk/cases/UKSC/2015/11.pdf

A doctor is under a duty to take reasonable care to ensure that a patient is aware of any material risks involved in any recommended treatment, and of any reasonable alternative or variant treatments. The test of materiality is whether, in the circumstances, a reasonable person in the patient's position would be likely to attach significance to the risk, or the doctor was or should reasonably be aware that the particular patient would be likely to attach significance to it.

This test takes into account the importance of personal autonomy and the value of self-determination and that, in making a decision which might have a profound effect on her health and well-being, a patient is entitled to information and advice about possible alternative and variant treatments.

In relation to patients who are competent to give consent, claims will rarely arise as to whether consent has been given. Claims do and will arise as to whether the information given by the clinician in obtaining consent was adequate. Consent and failure to warn are part of the same issue so far as the doctor's duty of care is concerned. Consent and the process of consenting is dealt with in Chapter 13 above.

Many professional bodies now provide detailed guidance for members on consent. See references to the GMC and RSC guidance in Chapter 13 above.

(iii)   The need for damages

At the beginning of this section (Civil Claims for Damages in Negligence) the requirements for establishing a claim were set out. Once negligence or a breach of duty is proved the claimant has to prove as well that that negligence or breach of duty caused some damage, injury or loss. Unless it did cause damage, injury or loss, there is no claim.

It is not unusual in clinical practice for a practitioner to recognise that there has been negligence – that her or a colleague's standard of care fell below that reasonably to be expected of a reasonably competent practitioner in that field – but that no adverse result occurred. In those circumstances there can be no claim in damages made, although there may be a requirement to report what happened as a serious incident (see Section 15.4 above) or it may become the subject of an investigation as to fitness to practise (see Section 15.7 below).

(iv)   Assessing damages

Once it is established that there has been a breach of duty that has caused injury or damage to the claimant, the legal principle underlying the assessment of compensation and an award of damages is known as the '100% Recovery Principle'[15]:

---

15   *Wells v Wells* [1999] 1 AC 345 at 382H, *Thompstone v Tameside & Glossop Acute Services* [2008] EWCA Civ 5

> *In settling the sum of money to be given for reparation of damages you should as nearly as possible get at that sum of money which will put the party who has been injured, or who has suffered, in the same position as he would have been in if he had not sustained the wrong for which he is now getting his compensation or reparation*[16].

This principle may be applied without great difficulty to past loss, where for example loss of earnings can be based on the earnings received immediately before the accident or on the earnings of a comparable employee and where expenses reasonably incurred can be proved with receipts. For future loss of earnings, in a straightforward case, the court can assess damages on the basis of the likely level of earnings along a probable career path. However, valuing damages for non-financial loss, such as a physical or psychological injury or the loss of ability to enjoy certain aspects of the claimant's pre-injury lifestyle, defies a truly logical approach[17].

Assessing the compensation necessary to achieve full and fair recovery in relation to losses that have not yet been incurred, such as future loss of earnings or future care, is often fraught with difficulty and may enter the realm of educated guesswork:

> *The object of the award of damages for future expenditure is to place the injured party as nearly as possible in the same financial position as he or she would have been in but for the accident. The aim is to award such a sum of money as will amount to no more, and at the same time no less, than the net loss*[18].

As a result, the parties will need to adduce evidence addressing not only what the consequences of an injury on the claimant's capabilities are and probably will be, but also what would probably have occurred in the claimant's life in the absence of the injury sustained. Both aspects are likely to be full of uncertainty, but the court will have to establish the probable scenarios and will almost certainly rely on expert opinion to achieve this.

Damages are recoverable where the result of negligence is the death of the patient. The deceased's estate may bring a claim (under the Law Reform (Miscellaneous Provisions) Act 1934 for the damages which the deceased could have recovered had he or she not died (usually in circumstances where the death does not follow immediately on from the negligence which caused it). Claims may also be made by a defined class of dependants of the deceased (under the Fatal Accidents Act 1976).

---

16   *Livingstone v Rawyards Coal Company* (1880) 5 App Cas 25 at 39

17   Assistance in the assessment of damages for pain and suffering and loss of amenity (general damages) is given in the Judicial College publication Guidelines for the assessment of general damages in personal injury cases (OUP) now in its 14th edition

18   *Wells v Wells* [1999] 1 AC 345 at 390A

15.6 Criminal prosecution

We will consider 4 different types of crimes for which a prosecution can be brought arising out of a clinical incident. It is unusual for a clinician or a healthcare provider to be charged with a crime, and generally it requires some exceptional circumstances to precipitate such action.

Being a criminal matter, the defendant is of course presumed innocent unless and until proved guilty, and proof must be 'beyond reasonable doubt' so that a jury is sure of guilt before convicting the defendant.

(i) Manslaughter by gross negligence[19]

A criminal prosecution may be brought in exceptional circumstances where a patient dies as a result of a clinician's failings. For such a conviction, which may well result in a significant prison sentence, the prosecution must prove to the criminal standard of proof (so that the jury is sure) each of the following, that:

1. The defendant was in breach of a duty of care owed to the victim. That is the same test as in civil claims and discussed in the previous section above.

2. The breach of that duty caused the death of the victim.

3. The circumstances of the breach were truly exceptionally bad and so reprehensible as to justify the conclusion that it amounted to gross negligence and required a criminal sanction.

    'Gross' negligence requires something more than a very serious mistake or error of judgment. The jury must be sure *'that the conduct of the clinician fell so far below the standard to be expected of a reasonably competent clinician of that type that his or her negligence should be characterised as gross in the sense that it was truly exceptionally bad and was such a departure from that standard that it consequently amounted to it being criminal ....'*[20]

4. It was reasonably foreseeable that the breach of that duty gave rise to a serious and obvious risk of death; and

    (i) that risk must exist at, and is to be assessed with respect to, knowledge at the time of the breach of duty

    (ii) a mere possibility that an assessment might reveal something life-threatening is not the same as an 'obvious risk of death': an 'obvious

---

19 In Scotland there is an offence of culpable homicide, not gross negligence, for the details of which readers will have to refer elsewhere.

20 *R v Sellu* [2016] EWCA Crim 1716, http://www.bailii.org/ew/cases/EWCA/Crim/2016/1716.html

risk' is a present risk which is clear and unambiguous, not one which might become apparent on further investigation.

In a case where an optometrist failed properly to examine the internal structure of a patient's eyes in a routine examination, the patient subsequently died as a consequence of an abnormality on the optic nerve which she had missed. There was the possibility that the signs of a life-threatening disease or abnormality might be missed but at the time of the breach of duty there was no serious and obvious risk of death. Therefore the conviction was overturned by the Court of Appeal[21].

Similarly in another case a GP advised the mother of a sick child on the telephone on a Friday evening to bring the child into surgery after the weekend. The child died in the early hours of Saturday. Experts agreed that the GP needed a face-to-face assessment of the child in order to fully assess the risk. Therefore there was no obvious and serious risk of death at the time of the advice on Friday and the charge of manslaughter could not be made out.

It should be noted that in both these cases there would be no doubt that a claim in negligence (applying *Bolam*) would succeed.

Punishment theoretically includes any period of imprisonment up to life although guidelines would indicate a sentence between 1 and 4 years' imprisonment.

Recent concerns about prosecution of clinicians for this offence has led to a report by Professor Sir Norman Williams (the *Williams Report*) with recommendations[22].

(ii)   Ill treatment or wilful neglect

After the Mid-Staffordshire NHS Foundation Trust inquiry, the government introduced a new crime in Section 20 of the Criminal Justice and Courts Act 2015 of 'ill-treatment or wilful neglect', greatly extending the reach of the criminal law into the practice of medicine.

The offence created is as follows:

> *It is an offence for an individual who has the care of another individual by virtue of being a care worker to ill-treat or wilfully to neglect that individual.*

The provision applies to anyone coming within the definition of 'care worker' in Section 20(3) of the Act: This provides that:-

---

21   *R v Rose* [2017] EWCA Crim 1168, http://www.bailii.org/ew/cases/EWCA/Crim/2017/1168.html

22   Gross negligence manslaughter in healthcare. The report of a rapid policy review (2018)

'Care worker' means an individual who, as paid work, provides—

(a) health care for an adult or child, other than excluded health care [not relevant for the purposes of this book], or

(b) social care for an adult, including an individual who, as paid work, supervises or manages individuals providing such care or is a director or similar officer of an organisation which provides such care.

'Health care' has a wide definition in Section 20(5) and includes—

all forms of health care provided for individuals, including health care relating to physical health or mental health and health care provided for or in connection with the protection or improvement of public health.

'Social care' is defined in Section 20(6) and includes –

all forms of personal care and other practical assistance provided for individuals who are in need of such care or assistance by reason of age, illness, disability, pregnancy, childbirth, dependence on alcohol or drugs or any other similar circumstances.

Therefore the offence is generally applicable to the work of all paid healthcare professionals in their work with adults and children in both physical and mental health care.

Punishment is provided for in Section 20(2)

An individual guilty of an offence under this section is liable—

(a) on conviction on indictment [i.e. for a more serious offence, dealt with in the Crown Court], to imprisonment for a term not exceeding 5 years or a fine (or both);

(b) on summary conviction [i.e. for a less serious offence, dealt with in the Magistrates' Court], to imprisonment for a term not exceeding 12 months or a fine (or both).

(iii)   Assault

For these purposes, an assault is any touching of another person that is unlawful. The touching will be unlawful unless there is consent (express or implied) or necessity. Without consent (express or implied) to a procedure and good reason, it is an assault to operate on a patient and even to lay hands on a patient. It is the consent (or in urgent cases, necessity) which makes the actions, otherwise an assault, lawful. A mentally competent patient has an absolute right to refuse consent to medical treatment for any reason, rational or irrational, or for no reason at all, even where that decision will lead to death[23].

There is no requirement to explain the 'possible major consequences' together with the 'options' and 'alternative treatments' in order to negative an assault arising out of a medical procedure; it is sufficient that the patient consents to the procedure having been advised in broad terms of its nature; even though a failure to advise as to the consequences or alternatives might expose the practitioner to a claim in negligence (see Section 15.5 above) it would not vitiate consent.

There are different offences of assault depending on whether harm is caused and the extent of that harm. Punishment depends on the category and seriousness of the assault and at the most serious end includes imprisonment for life.

Common assault

It is an offence to assault someone unlawfully even if there is no actual harm caused, under Section 39 of the Criminal Justice Act 1988. Further, although no visible injury is caused and although no harm is done, it is an assault to mark an internal organ for purposes unrelated to the surgery being carried out[24].

Assault occasioning actual bodily harm

It is an offence to assault someone thereby causing them actual bodily harm. For these purposes a person is guilty of an assault occasioning actual bodily harm under Section 47 of the Offences Against the Person Act 1861 if she does an act intentionally or recklessly which causes the victim to sustain unlawful personal violence and the assault caused actual bodily harm. Recklessly means that the assailant foresaw the possibility that the victim would sustain that violence and nevertheless took that risk. Unlawful means that there is no lawful justification for the violence such as self-defence, consent or necessity. Actual bodily harm means what it says. It includes any hurt or injury calculated to interfere with the health or comfort of the victim and need not be permanent although it must be more than merely transient or trifling. It may be psychiatric injury but not merely fear, distress or panic.

Assault causing grievous bodily harm or wounding

If more serious injury is caused, then there are offences of assault causing grievous bodily harm or wounding, under Section 18 of the Offences Against the Person Act 1861 if with intent to cause such grievous bodily harm, or under Section 20 in the absence of such an intent. 'Grievous bodily harm' means really serious bodily harm.

---

23   Re J.T. (Adult: Refusal of Medical Treatment) [1998] 1 F.L.R. 48, Fam D and Re B. (adult: refusal of medical treatment) [2002] 2 All E.R. 449, Fam D

24   R v Bramhall (December 2017)

(v)   Health & safety

While it is not uncommon to find prosecutions against a healthcare provider under the Health and Safety at Work Act 1974 in relation to accidents involving employees of the healthcare provider, prosecutions are also possible in relation to the care of patients.

Section 3(1) of the Act imposes a duty to conduct the undertaking in such a way as to ensure, as far as is reasonably practicable, the safety of persons not in employment but who may be affected by it. In *R v Southern Health NHS Foundation Trust*[25] the NHS Trust pleaded guilty to 2 offences. The first was exposing a very disturbed and vulnerable patient, with a history of self-harm and suicidal ideation, in a psychiatric ward to a ligature risk in the form of a telephone cord on a pay phone which was out of clear view of staff, and which the patient used as a ligature to suspend herself from. The second concerned a young man who suffered from learning disability, autism and epilepsy and who drowned in a bath in an assessment centre. In both cases there was a lack of a coherent risk assessment of the patient.

Although this was an extreme case (the NHS Trust was fined £2million) criminal charges can result from a lack of proper risk assessments of patients and their environment.

15.7 Fitness to practise

Each healthcare regulator has its own rules and procedures. The GMC acts under the Medical Act 1983 and its Fitness to Practise Rules 2004 (amended in March 2013). But there are features common to all of the professional bodies. We deal here primarily with the GMC process.

(i)   Impaired fitness to practise

In the case of the GMC, Section 35C of the Medical Act 1983 states that a person's fitness to practise shall be regarded as impaired by reason only of—

(a) Misconduct

(b) Deficient professional performance

(c) A conviction or caution for a criminal offence

(d) Adverse physical or mental health

(e) A determination by a regulatory body that fitness to practise as a member of that profession is impaired

---

25   https://www.judiciary.gov.uk/wp-content/uploads/2018/03/r-v-southern-nhs-sentencing.pdf

(f) Not having the necessary knowledge of English.

'Misconduct' means nothing less than 'serious professional misconduct'. And such misconduct, although it may relate to professional misconduct, is not limited to that context. Incompetence or negligence of a high degree – gross professional negligence - may amount to such misconduct. A single act of negligence or negligent omission is less likely to amount to misconduct than multiple acts or omissions.

Similarly, 'deficient professional performance' refers to a standard of professional performance which is unacceptably low and a single instance of negligent treatment is unlikely to suffice, unless it is very serious indeed.

A report prepared on the complaints resulting in erasure or suspension from the medical register in 2014[26] provides a snapshot of the professional conduct of concern in process that concluded that year, although it is not itself evidence of any general trend:

> The majority of cases were in relation to an incident in a doctor's working life, although some were in relation to a doctor's personal life. The latter category involved fairly extreme cases and particular those involving sexual issues (which ranged from voyeurism to sexual assault) but also offences of drink driving, and incidents of dishonesty and violence.
>
> Overall, the most common type of case was dishonesty. In decreasing order of occurrence, they related to: obtaining or keeping employment, such as in relation to qualifications or suitability, including false CVs and references; dishonesty during the fitness to practise process, such as failing to disclose the investigation or conditions imposed by the GMC to an employer or over identity or the right to work; falsifying what had been done at work, such as false claims about work; or in relation to prescriptions.
>
> The second most common type of case was inappropriate relations with both patients and colleagues, the former being more common.
>
> The third most common type of case was clinical issues although a proportion of these cases also involved dishonesty.
>
> A further small number of varied cases were classified as 'breaking other professional standards'.

---

26   Analysis of cases resulting in doctors being erased or suspended from the medical register: Report prepared for: General Medical Council October 2015 (Rebecca Harris, Kate Slater, DJS Research) https://www.gmc-uk.org/-/media/documents/Analysis_of_cases_resulting_in_doctors_being_suspended_or_erased_from_the_medical_register_FINAL_REPORT_Oct_2015.pdf_63534317.pdf

The different healthcare regulators publish guidance on their approach to what indicates deficient professional performance (see further reading below).

(ii)   Process

Investigation

An allegation against a member of a professional body will first be screened to see if it falls within the relevant definition(s) of impaired fitness to practise. If it is considered that the complaint does not fall within the definition of impaired fitness to practise, the person complained against ('the practitioner') may never hear about it. The GMC Registrar also has power to conclude the case on the grounds that it is vexatious. Otherwise it will be investigated. Even if the practitioner considers that the complaint is in fact groundless or malicious, that cannot be established without some investigation by the professional body. Therefore, co-operation with the process and a carefully reasoned answer to the complaint is almost certain to be the best approach, whatever may be the feelings about the complainant and his or her motivation.

The practitioner will receive information as to the allegations made which raise a question as to fitness to practise being impaired, and will be provided with copies of any documents supplied by the complainant in support of the allegation, with an invitation to respond in writing within a specified time. That response will normally be made available to the complainant. The GMC has power to direct the practitioner to undergo a health or performance assessment or assessment of her knowledge of English, in which case a copy of the assessment report will be supplied to her.

On receipt of the notification letter the practitioner must consider who needs to be informed of the allegation (employer, partners) and consider any insurance policy or professional indemnity agreement. Generally, insurers and indemnity bodies need to be informed as soon as a possible claim arises. Even if it is hoped to deal with the matter without professional assistance, if subsequently legal support is required, the cost will not be covered if there is late notification of the claim, even if at the end of the process the complaint is dismissed.

Complaints based on events more than 5 years old cannot form the basis of disciplinary proceedings at the GMC save in exceptional circumstances.

Under the GMC rules, after the complaint has been investigated a decision is made as to whether the allegation should not proceed further or a warning should be issued to the practitioner or whether the allegation should be referred to the Fitness to Practise Panel, in which case it is referred to the Medical Practitioners Tribunal Service ('MPTS'). Allegations will only be referred to the Panel for adjudication if there is a realistic prospect of establishing that the practitioner's fitness to practise is impaired to a degree justifying action on registration.

Although it may be an anonymous complaint that sets off an investigation by the professional body, a referral to a panel will require evidence of a nature which can be properly tested in cross-examination, and that will usually require the identity of the complainant to be known to the practitioner.

Hearing

The procedure before a professional tribunal is adversarial – it is not for the tribunal to investigate the evidence but for the parties to produce evidence, call witnesses and question witnesses. The prosecutor, that is the professional body, must prove the practitioner's guilt. The standard of proof is the civil standard of the balance of probabilities. Therefore, the facts upon which the complaint is based must be proved on the evidence produced before the tribunal as being more likely than not. This is in sharp contrast to the criminal standard of proof 'beyond reasonable doubt' or 'so that you are sure'.

Prior to the hearing, both the allegations made against the practitioner and the facts on which they are based will be particularised. The members of the tribunal will be identified so that they can be challenged should there be any risk of actual or perceived bias on their part. While the standard of proof is that of the civil courts, the procedure adopted by the GMC is largely that of the criminal courts. This includes, for example, the rule that hearsay evidence may be admissible only in certain circumstances (see Section 3.1(ii) for an explanation of hearsay).

Tribunals provide useful guidance as to their procedure, as in *Information for doctors* published by the MPTS (see below).

Hearings generally fall into 3 parts.

>Firstly the facts must be established (on the balance of probabilities) to the extent that they are not admitted by the practitioner.

>Secondly, the tribunal must exercise its judgment as to whether the facts which have been proved show that fitness to practise is impaired. If impairment is not found, the panel can still give a warning.

>Thirdly, if impairment is found, the tribunal moves on to decide on the appropriate sanction. The practitioner and the professional body can both call further relevant evidence at the second and third stages and make representations to the panel.

(iii)   Sanction

In the case of the GMC a complaint if proved may be resolved by the panel taking undertakings (as to future conduct) or imposing a sanction, which may involve imposing conditions, suspending or erasure from the medical register. The GMC and the MPTS provide guidance on sanctions (see below).

There is a right to appeal, within certain time limits, against a sanction to the High Court.

The recent high-profile case of Dr Bawa-Garba[27] raised the issue of the appropriate sanction in a case where a doctor was convicted of gross negligence manslaughter following a series of mistakes in difficult circumstances but with fatal consequences for the patient and the role of the MPTS.

Details of useful publications are given below.

Support for doctors can be obtained from the BMA's Doctor Support Service which produces a useful leaflet[28]. In addition, the professional indemnity organisations will provide advice, support and assistance.

15.8 Inquests

An inquest is a legal investigation to establish the circumstances surrounding a person's death, including how, when and why the death occurred. The inquest is carried out by a judicial officer, a lawyer with appropriate training, and is held in public in a coroner's court. An inquest is not concerned with establishing who was responsible for a person's death. It is a fact-finding exercise and no formal allegations will be made, and unlike court and most other proceedings, it is not adversarial, but inquisitorial. There is no prosecution, claimant or defence.

(i)   Involving the coroner

A doctor, rather than signing a medical certificate, may report the death to a coroner if:-

- The cause of death is unknown
- The death was violent or unnatural
- The death was sudden and unexplained
- The person who died was not visited by a medical practitioner during their final illness
- The medical certificate isn't available
- The person who died wasn't seen by the doctor who signed the medical certificate within 14 days before death or after they died
- The death occurred during an operation or before the person came out of anaesthetic
- The medical certificate suggests the death may have been caused by an industrial disease or industrial poisoning.

The doctor should record the details of referral to the coroner, and the reasons for it, in the patient's records.

---

27   https://www.bailii.org/ew/cases/EWCA/Civ/2018/1879.html

28   https://www.bma.org.uk/advice/work-life-support/your-wellbeing/doctor-support-service

The coroner may decide that the cause of death is clear or that a post-mortem is necessary. If the cause of death is, in the opinion of the coroner, still unknown, or if the person may have died a violent or unnatural death, or was in state detention (including under the Mental Health Act) then an inquest must be held. It is also usual, although not mandatory, for a coroner to hold an inquest where death has occurred within 24 hours of admission to hospital or of a surgical procedure. Even if death is due to natural causes, a coroner may hold an inquest if it is regarded as being in the public interest.

(ii)   Process

Generally, an inquest will be opened soon after the death to allow the death to be recorded, the deceased to be identified and for authorisation to be given by the coroner for burial or cremation. It will then be adjourned while investigations are completed.

Normally the coroner carries out the inquest alone but in certain limited circumstances a jury will be called to give a verdict.

At the inquest witnesses chosen by the coroner will give factual evidence based on a witness statement which will have been prepared previously. If a doctor's evidence is not controversial it may be accepted simply in the form of a report and the maker will not be called to give evidence. If a witness is called to give evidence, the coroner will ask questions to summarise the witness's evidence and to clarify matters in it. The coroner will then permit anyone with a 'proper interest', such as a family member of the deceased or anyone whose actions the coroner believes may have contributed to the death, or their representative, to ask questions. Witnesses may be represented by lawyers.

Questions are limited under Rule 36 of the Coroner's Rules to the issues of:-

1.   who the deceased was;

2.   how, when and where the deceased came by his death;

3.   the particulars required for registering the death.

'How' normally means simply 'by what means' but in certain circumstances, where there is potentially gross negligence, as opposed to ordinary medical negligence, or where the deceased was subject to compulsory hospital detention, the meaning of 'how' is extended to include the circumstances of death and to permit a wider reaching inquiry[29].

Evidence is given by witnesses under oath, as in a court or fitness to practise tribunal. The role of the coroner's court is one of investigation and inquiry and

---

29   This is the impact of Article 2 of the European Convention on Human Rights, a so-called 'Middleton' inquest.

it is not a function of the coroner to apportion blame. However, questions from family members of a deceased person can be hostile. As interested persons family members have the right to representation and therefore the questions may well be asked by lawyers.

An NHS trust may arrange legal representation to protect its own interests. Depending on the circumstances and any potential conflict of interest, the trust may also be able to represent practitioners employed by the trust. A self-employed practitioner, such as a practitioner in general practice or in private practice, will need to seek representation through a medical defence organisation or insurer. Similarly, where there is a potential conflict of interest between an NHS trust and an employee practitioner, the practitioner will need to seek independent representation.

(iii)   Verdict, standard of proof and outcomes

The coroner's verdict will include a statement about the cause of death and may also include a 'narrative' conclusion setting out the facts surrounding the death and explaining the reasons for the decision. The causes of death that will be recorded will include:

- natural causes
- accident or misadventure
- alcohol or drug related
- industrial disease
- unlawful killing
- open (a death that's suspicious but where it isn't possible to confirm the exact cause)
- suicide.

The standard of proof is the normal civil standard of the balance of probabilities, except possibly in relation to unlawful killing. The Court of Appeal has recently ruled that the normal civil standard of proof applies in the case of a verdict of suicide, contrary to previous practice, and although not expressly addressing a verdict of unlawful killing, which has hitherto required proof on the criminal standard (beyond reasonable doubt), throws doubt on that too[30]. (See Chapter 4 'Proof' above.)

The coroner does not decide issues of clinical negligence; however, the phrase 'aggravated by self-neglect or lack of care' can be added to the first four verdicts set out above - natural causes, accident or misadventure, alcohol or drug related or industrial disease - if it is appropriate. This may have implications for the healthcare professional involved.

The coroner can refer doctors to their regulatory body if the coroner considers that it would prevent a recurrence of the incident that caused the death.

---

30   *R v Kelly Shakespeare and others* [2018] EWHC 1955

There is an obligation on a doctor to inform the GMC immediately where there has been criticism by an official inquiry, which includes a coroner's inquest[31].

For all of these reasons if a doctor is concerned as to possible criticism at a coroner's inquest then the relevant medical defence organisation or insurer should be contacted for advice at the earliest opportunity.

The coroner's verdict can only be challenged by judicial review in the High Court, but this must be within three months of the conclusion of the inquest.

15.9 Disciplinary proceedings

NHS organisations are required to have procedures for handling concerns about the conduct, performance and health of medical and dental employees (generally excluding those who perform PCT Medical Services). Local procedures are required to be in accordance with the framework set out in *Maintaining High Professional Standards in the Modern NHS* (2003, amended 2005)[32].

An employer will have a code of conduct or a set of staff rules setting out acceptable standards of conduct and behaviour applicable to all staff. Breaches of these rules will be regarded as misconduct, and this will generally, but not exclusively, come into one of the following categories:

- A refusal to comply with the reasonable requirements of an employer
- An infringement of the employer's disciplinary rules including conduct that contravenes the standard of professional behaviour required of doctors and dentists by their regulatory body
- The commission of criminal offences outside the place of work which may, in particular circumstances, amount to misconduct
- Wilful, careless, inappropriate or unethical behaviour likely to compromise standards of care or patient safety, or create serious dysfunction to the effective running of a service.

Verbal or physical bullying, harassment and discrimination in the exercise of a practitioner's duties towards patients, the public or other employees, as also actions such as deliberate falsification or fraud, will all amount to misconduct. A failure to fulfil contractual obligations may amount to misconduct, such as failure to attend at clinics or ward rounds, or failing properly to support other members of staff. The most serious acts will amount to gross misconduct and may justify summary dismissal.

In relation to issues of capability, there are 4 main themes underlying the framework:

---

31   Good Medical Practice (GMC) para 75a

32   Under the Restriction of Practice and Exclusion from Work Directions 2003, and the Directions on Disciplinary Procedures 2004. The Framework can be found at http://webarchive. nationalarchives.gov.uk/20130123204228/http://www.dh.gov.uk/en/Publicationsandstatistics/Publications/PublicationsPolicyAndGuidance/DH_4103586

- Appraisal and revalidation - processes which encourage practitioners to maintain the skills and knowledge needed for their work through continuing professional development
  Appraisal is a structured process which gives doctors an opportunity to reflect on their practice and discuss, with a suitably trained and qualified appraiser, any issues arising from their work, and their development needs. Appraisal is a contractual requirement for NHS consultants and GP Principals.
- The advisory and assessment services of the National Clinical Assessment Service (NCAS) - aimed at enabling NHS Trusts to handle cases quickly and fairly reducing the need to use disciplinary procedures to resolve problem
- Tackling the blame culture - recognising that most failures in standards of care are caused by systems' weaknesses and not individuals per se
- Abandoning the 'suspension culture' - by introducing the new arrangements for handling exclusion from work set out in part II of the framework.

Procedures are required in NHS organisations when 'serious concerns' about an individual's conduct and capability are raised. A 'serious concern' is one where the practitioner's actions have or may adversely affect patient care.

When a serious concern is raised about a practitioner:

1. The employer must urgently consider whether it is necessary to place temporary restrictions on the practitioner's practice, such as to amend or restrict clinical duties, obtain undertakings or exclude the practitioner from the workplace.

2. If the case manager appointed by the organisation's medical director considers that the practitioner is a serious potential danger to patients or staff, then the practitioner must be referred to the regulatory body (GMC or GDC).

The case manager's first task is to identify the nature of the concern to assess its seriousness and consider with the medical director the likelihood that it can be resolved without resort to formal disciplinary procedures. Where a formal route leading to conduct or capability proceedings is considered appropriate, an appropriately experienced person will be appointed as case investigator. The case investigator will then ensure that sufficient evidence in written statements is collected to establish a case before any decision is made to convene a disciplinary panel. It is emphasised that investigations may support a complaint or exonerate a practitioner or provide a basis for effective resolution of the matter.

The healthcare organisation may seek advice from the National Clinical Assessment Service (NCAS) about all aspects of a practitioner's performance and also if consideration is being given to excluding, suspending or restricting a practitioner's practice. An NHS organisation must contact NCAS if formal exclusion is being considered in relation to an employed doctor or salaried dentist, or if the healthcare organisation is considering taking action in relation to an employed practitioner under the capability procedures referred to below and an assessment is to be undertaken, or if an NHS body is seeking the issue of a Healthcare Professionals Alert Notice.

The practitioner will be informed in writing by the case manager as soon as it is decided that an investigation is to be undertaken, and will be told the name of the case investigator and the specific allegations or concerns raised, together with the opportunity to see any correspondence in relation to the case and a list of the people that the case investigator will interview. The practitioner will then be given the opportunity to put his or her views to the case investigator, and is entitled to be accompanied by someone when doing so.

In a case involving complex clinical issues, the case manager may appoint an independent practitioner from another NHS body to assist.

There is a timetable for the investigation, which should be complete in 4 weeks and reported to the case manager within a further 5 days.

There is a requirement that employers must maintain confidentiality at all times, and that the name of any practitioner being investigated should not be released.

Exclusion from work of a practitioner can only be used as an interim measure while the complaint is being considered, is a precautionary measure and not a sanction, and must be for the minimum necessary time and for no more than 4 weeks at a time between reviews. It should be reserved for only the most exceptional circumstances and in order to protect the interests of staff or patients or to assist the investigative process where the practitioner's presence would impede the gathering of evidence.

Misconduct matters will be dealt with under the procedures covering all staff charged with similar matters. Professional misconduct matters require the case investigator obtaining appropriate independent professional advice, and if the matter proceeds to a hearing the panel must include a medically (or, in appropriate cases, dentally) qualified member not currently employed by the NHS organisation.

15.10 Care quality commission inspections

The Care Quality Commission carries out comprehensive inspections and generally unannounced focused inspections to look at specific matters of concern or where there has been a change in the care provider's circumstances.

Such inspections involve gathering the views of people who use services in a variety of ways, gathering information from staff and observing care, reviewing records, inspecting the places where people are cared for, and looking at documents and policies. There are a range of inspection frameworks for different organisations, all available on the CQC website.

For example, and to give an indication of the nature of inquiries made in such inspections, the framework for hospital and ambulance core services[33] lists a series of frameworks including that for 'NHS Hospitals: surgery'. This provides guidance under the following headings of areas to be looked at:

Safety

> *Are lessons learned and improvements made when things go wrong?*
>
> *What is the track record on safety?*
>
> *Are there reliable systems, processes and practices in place to keep people safe and safeguarded from abuse?*
>
> *How are risks to people who use services assessed, and their safety monitored and maintained?*
>
> *How well are potential risks to the service anticipated and planned for in advance?*

Effectiveness

> *Are people's needs assessed and care and treatment delivered in line with legislation, standards and evidence-based guidance?*
>
> *How are people's care and treatment outcomes monitored and how do they compare with other services?*
>
> *Do staff have the skills, knowledge and experience to deliver effective care and treatment?*
>
> *How well do staff, teams and services work together to deliver effective care and treatment?*
>
> *Do staff have all the information they need to deliver effective care and treatment to people who use services?*
>
> *Is people's consent to care and treatment always sought in line with legislation and guidance?*

Caring

> *Are people treated with kindness, dignity, respect and compassion*

33　https://www.cqc.org.uk/guidance-providers/how-we-inspect-regulate/inspection-frame-works-hospital-ambulance-core-services *while they receive care and treatment?*

Are people who use services and those close to them involved as partners in their care?

Do people who use services and those close to them receive the support they need to cope emotionally with their care, treatment or condition?

Responsiveness

Do people who use services and those close to them receive the support they need to cope emotionally with their care, treatment or condition?

Do services take account of the needs of different people, including those in vulnerable circumstances?

Can people access care and treatment in a timely way?

How are people's concerns and complaints listened and responded to and used to improve the quality of care?

Well led

Is there a clear vision and a credible strategy to deliver good quality?

Does the governance framework ensure that responsibilities are clear and that quality, performance and risks are understood and managed?

How does the leadership and culture reflect the vision and values, encourage openness and transparency and promote good quality care?

How are people who use the service, the public and staff engaged and involved?

How are services continuously improved and sustainability ensured?

The CQC has a range of enforcement powers, including prosecution for breach of Regulations (see for example the CQC *Enforcement Policy*[34]).

---

34   https://www.cqc.org.uk/sites/default/files/20150209_enforcement_policy_v1-1.pdf

15.11 Insurance, indemnity and support

You must make sure that you have adequate insurance or indemnity cover so that your patients will not be disadvantaged if they make a claim about the clinical care you have provided in the UK[35].

Not only is it a professional requirement to have adequate insurance or indemnity cover but in addition since July 2014 under the Health Care and Associated Professions (Indemnity Arrangements) Order 2014 all registered healthcare professionals are legally required to have adequate and appropriate insurance or indemnity to cover the different aspects of their practice in the UK. Further the GMC can:

- *check that any doctor practising in the UK has adequate and appropriate insurance or indemnity cover*
- *remove a doctor's licence to stop them from practising altogether, if we learn that they don't have adequate and appropriate insurance or indemnity or if they fail to give us the information we ask for*
- *refuse to grant a licence to a doctor if they can't assure us that they'll have the adequate and appropriate insurance or indemnity by the time they start practising in the UK[36].*

In any event it is clearly sound business sense as well as an absolute professional requirement to have suitable insurance (or indemnity) cover in place for all aspects of a healthcare professional's work to pay out in the case of any negligence on the part of the practitioner causing injury or loss. For present purposes we can treat indemnity and insurance as the same – they have the same affect for the clinician in that they pay up if a claim is made against the clinician, but both the NHS and medical defence bodies in fact provide indemnity.

For work carried out by medical or dental staff under their employment contract with an NHS trust, practitioners are covered by the NHS indemnity scheme ('Crown Indemnity') and therefore it is not necessary to hold indemnity insurance (for example through membership of a defence society) for such work. However, many services that healthcare professionals may commonly provide are not covered because they are not within the NHS contract. Examples are:

- providing reports outside of the practitioner's contractual duties, including reports on patients for courts, insurance companies, state benefit claims
- appearing at court as a factual witness
- expert witness work
- Category 3 work including under a waiting list initiative
- Category 2 work which is work which is not principally to do with the prevention, diagnosis and treatment of illness and for which a fee can

---

35   Good Medical Practice (GMC) para 63

36   https://www.gmc-uk.org/registration-and-licensing/managing-your-registration/information-for-doctors-on-the-register/insurance-indemnity-and-medico-legal-support

usually be requested from a body outside the health service.

For all of these, insurance (or indemnity) cover is necessary and essential. It is therefore important to understand what the NHS contractual duties are. A useful guide to work within and without the NHS indemnity scheme is provided by the BMA[37].

Further it should be noted that the NHS indemnity scheme does not cover general practitioners except for work under a trust's contract of employment (as for example as a hospital practitioner or a clinical assistant).

Membership of a defence society, such as the MPS and MDU, is therefore strongly advised, in order to ensure that all activities are covered. For those carrying out private work it is essential. Defence body subscriptions are allowable against tax.

It should also be understood that the NHS indemnity scheme does not cover work defending medical staff in GMC or other professional conduct proceedings. Nor does it cover 'good Samaritan' acts (eg 'is there a doctor on the plane?'), work for charities or work overseas. For these purposes again membership of a defence organisation is essential.

There are three medical defence organisations in the UK: Medical Defence Union (MDU), Medical Protection Society (MPS) and Medical and Dental Defence Union of Scotland (MDDUS). They offer different membership benefits. They are non-profit making organisations owned by their members which in addition to providing indemnity also provide members with 24-hour access to advice and assistance on medico-legal issues arising from clinical practice. There are few insurance providers in the market place.

---

37   The BMA's Guidance Note on the NHS indemnity scheme can be found at https://www.
bma.org.uk/-/media/files/pdfs/practical%20advice%20at%20work/contracts/nhsmedicalin-
demnity.pdf?la=en

Further reading

Openness and honesty when things go wrong: the professional duty of candour (GMC and NMC)[38]

Raising and acting on concerns about patient safety (GMC)[39]

Voicing your concerns for Staff (whistleblowing policy) (NHS England)[40]

Guide to raising concerns (BMA)[41]

Serious Incident Framework – frequently asked questions (NHS England)[42]

Gross negligence manslaughter in healthcare. The report of a rapid policy review (2018)[43]

The meaning of fitness to practise (GMC)[44]

Ensuring public safety, enabling professionalism (NMC)[45]

Fitness to Practise: What does it mean? (HCPC)[46]

Sanction Guidance (GMC)[47]

Guidance to the GMC's Fitness to Practise Rules 2004 (as amended)[48]

Information for doctors whose cases are due to be heard by a fitness to practise panel (MPTS)[49]

---

38 https://www.gmc-uk.org/static/documents/content/DoC_guidance_english.pdf

39 https://www.gmc-uk.org/static/documents/content/Raising_and_acting_on_concerns_about_patient_safety_-_English_1015.pdf

40 https://www.england.nhs.uk/wp-content/uploads/2016/09/voicing-concerns-staff-policy.pdf

41 https://www.bma.org.uk/advice/employment/raising-concerns/guide-to-raising-concerns

42 https://improvement.nhs.uk/uploads/documents/serious-incdnt-framwrk-faqs-mar16.pdf

43 https://assets.publishing.service.gov.uk/government/uploads/system/uploads/attachment_data/file/717946/Williams_Report.pdf

44 https://www.gmc-uk.org/-/media/documents/DC4591_The_meaning_of_fitness_to_practise_25416562.pdf

45 https://www.nmc.org.uk/globalassets/sitedocuments/consultations/2018/ftp/ensuringpublicsafety_v6.pdf

46 http://www.hcpc-uk.co.uk/assets/documents/10002FD8FTP_What_does_it_mean.pdf

47 https://www.mpts-uk.org/DC4198_Sanctions_Guidance_Feb_2018_23008260.pdf

48 https://www.gmc-uk.org/DC4483_Guidance_to_the_FTP_Rules_28626691.pdf

49 www.mpts-uk.org

General Medical Council (Fitness to Practise) Rules Order of Council 2004[50]

The Regulation of Healthcare Professionals: Law, Principle and Process - Glyn & Gomez (Sweet & Maxwell 2012)

Disciplinary and Regulatory Proceedings - Harris & Carnes (Jordan 2013)

Coroner investigations: a short guide[51]

FAQs at the Coroners' Society[52]

Fact sheet on Inquests (MPS)[53]

---

50   https://www.mpts-uk.org/consolidated_version_of_FTP_Rules.dec2015.pdf_64002624.pdf

51   https://www.gov.uk/government/uploads/system/uploads/attachment_data/file/283937/ coroner-investigations-a-short-guide.pdf

52   https://www.coronersociety.org.uk/faqs/

53   http://www.medicalprotection.org/docs/default-source/pdfs/factsheet-pdfs/england-fact-sheet-pdfs/inquests.pdf?sfvrsn=9

Lightning Source UK Ltd.
Milton Keynes UK
UKHW020739030619

343780UK00005B/945/P